RUGS
to Riches

THE AMAZING STORY
OF THE

DUSTY & BONNIE HENSON

TREGO-HILL PUBLICATION
EL PASO • TEXAS

FIRST EDITION
Revised and expanded

10   9   8   7   6   5

Publisher's Cataloging-in-Publication Data

    Henson, Dusty
        Rugs to Riches, The Amazing Story of El Paso Saddleblanket / by
        Dusty Henson and Bonnie Henson. – 1st edition.
            p.   cm.
            LCCN: 01-135493
            ISBN-10: 0-9636577-9-8 / ISBN-13: 978-0-9636577-9-4
        1. Business. 2. Sales and Marketing. 3. Arts.
    I. Title.

Book design, cover design & typesetting by Vicki Trego Hill of El Paso, Texas
Edited by John William Byrd of El Paso, Texas
Printed and bound in the U.S.A. by McNaughton & Gunn, Inc.

Contents

ACKNOWLEDGEMENTS

Thanks to Vicki Trego Hill for a fantastic design, John William Byrd for his editing expertise, McNaughton & Gunn for the printing, Peggy Rosson for her fond memories of our political antics, and Bill Crawford for helping us organize our thoughts, writings and memories into a coherent book.

Most of all, thanks to our employees past and present at El Paso Saddleblanket Company. Y'all are truly amazing.

To ALL THE FRIENDS *(and enemies) we have made over four decades of trading.*

Introduction

"Always, always, look 'em in the eyes, do a big smile,
and say thank you when you give 'em change,
cause if they like you, they'll come back later
and be your repeat customers."

—My father, Mack Henson, 1950

 My friends have often asked me, "Dusty, when are you going to write your story?" Well, here it is and it's nothing fancy. I didn't become successful because of any invention, fad, discovery, stroke of luck, pedigree or contacts from the Wharton School of Business. I'm just an average guy who took an average business and did better than average by working hard and doing *almost* all the right things; an old boy from Abilene, Texas who got out and knocked on some doors and sold some stuff. It isn't brain surgery, but it sure has been fun!

I guess if I have a particular skill or genius, it is trade. I was born to trade. Ever since I was a kid in school I've been trading. It didn't matter what I traded, just as long as I could buy it and sell it.

I've never had a salaried job, except for the U.S. Army and the ten days I spent working for Gibson's Department Store when I was in college.

No matter how hard the times got, there was just something in me that wanted to stay independent and keep trading. I've been lucky that my trading has led to a great business—and a great marriage. Best of all, my life as a trader has allowed me to travel and really understand other cultures, especially Mexico.

I have lived either in or very near Mexico all of my adult life. My home in El Paso is about a mile from the Rio Grande River and the international boundary line. Founded some four hundred years ago, El Paso is the oldest town in Texas and was originally called Paso del Norte (Pass of the North). From my upstairs bedroom, I can see the historic pass cut by the Rio Grande. The pass marks the end of the Rocky Mountains at the base of Mt. Franklin near downtown El Paso, and the beginning of the Sierra Madre Mountains which rise up on the other side of the Rio Grande and extend south into Mexico.

El Paso/Juárez is the largest city in the world on a bilingual border, and I love the *bordertown* mentality here. Throughout history, El Paso has attracted outlaws, gunfighters, gamblers, and hustlers. Even today, folks in town are uncomfortable when people start asking too many personal questions. We have a higher tolerance of characters than the rest of Texas, perhaps because non-Hispanics only make up eighteen percent of the population. We usually speak Spanish in El Paso, and we definitely prefer tortillas to bread.

I know that you've all seen pictures of the horn of plenty, the cone shaped basket with all the fruit flowing out of the top. Many Mexicans say this is very symbolic to them in that the basket is shaped like Mexico, and all the beautiful fruit resembles the United States. To me, the horn of plenty has looked just the opposite: I've always seen the fruit when looking south.

El Paso Saddleblanket Company was born when I began hawking blankets woven in Mexico out of the back of a pick-up. Today, more than forty years later, El Paso Saddleblanket is a multi-million dollar operation, based in a huge, one-acre showroom with three acres of free parking, located in central El Paso on freeway frontage. We mail out 250,000 color catalogs every ninety days plus special catalogs twice a year. We maintain an internet newsletter and an online trading site, which is becoming an important part of our business.

I've dealt with thousands of people over the years—old timers in horse carts, trading post owners along Route 66, gallery owners, desert rats, every kind of gypsy road warrior in the world. I like to shoot a straight deal to a straight guy, make a little bit and let him make some. That's the way I've been trading for more than forty years, and it still works for me.

One thing I know for sure—you'll never be a successful world trader if you have racial, religious or ethnic prejudices. If you want to be a bigot, go hate who you want, but don't try to be a trader. You can't last in this business if you hate any racial, ethnic, or religious group.

Times have changed since I started trading. It's not like it used to be in Mexico, or anywhere else in the world for that matter. It's taken me most of my lifetime to build up my wholesale business, and if I had to start over again, I don't know if I could make it.

My business has never really been about the money. Sure, I've done well, but I have never worked just for the money's sake. Yes, money is a score card, and I usually have winning years. I have turned rugs into riches—not big riches, but at least enough to let me live comfortably. But the truly valuable riches of my business lie in the experiences I have had all over the world, the friends I have made, and the wonderful products I have been able to deliver to my customers.

In this book you'll meet some wild characters and learn about my adventures around the world, most of them profitable. You'll get a chance to find out about my wife and business partner, Bonnie Henson, and read some of her observations about business and travel. Along the way, you'll pick up on some of the valuable lessons we've learned about doing business, lessons that will help you make your own business a success. Because no matter what business you're in, it all comes down to making the trade.

PART 1
Born to Trade

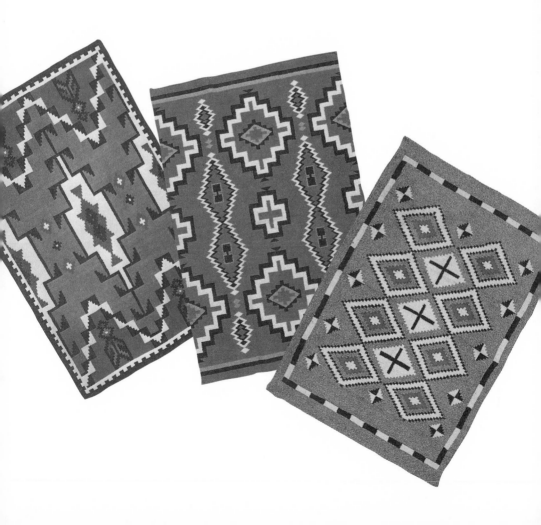

Chapter One

The Natural

"Trading is a lot like tending a flock. Your customers are your sheep. You can shear them every year, but you can only skin them once."

—MACK HENSON, 1950

 AS LONG AS I CAN REMEMBER I've wanted to be a trader. As a little kid, one of my favorite games was to drag out all the canned goods from the cupboard and play store. I was never much of a mathematical whiz, but I was proud that I knew how to make change before the other kids my age did.

I grew up in Abilene, Texas, in the part of town that lay north of the railroad line that came through in 1881. The south side was richer than the north side, but our neighborhood had a real mix of all kinds of people and good, safe schools.

One thing I noticed early on was that if you had a little money, you could buy all the other kids ice cream and everybody would like you. That presented the problem of how to get extra money over and above my small allowance.

One of the first things I did was to get into the donkey business. I had a donkey and used to let the other kids ride. For the small kids who couldn't ride by themselves, I'd lead the donkey myself, for a small fee.

One day I noticed that all new pencils were sawed off flat on the end and were not sharpened. That gave me a brilliant idea. If I took a sharpened pencil and sawed it off flat, it would be a "new" pencil. To me the length didn't matter just as long as it was cut off smooth at the end. Pencils were always available for the asking (so long as they were for school), and I began asking for them, cutting off the ends and selling them to other kids. The older kids began to question the fact that these were the shortest new pencils they had ever seen. They noticed that the shortest of the short had erasers that appeared to be used. I told them that the short pencils were made that way to fit behind the ear! Even though I took some teasing, I realized that my new enterprise was all profit. I was proud of myself.

IN THE SUMMER OF 1954, I started making some of my first really successful trades from behind the plywood counter of a sno-cone stand. As in any retail business, the secret of my success was location. My stand was in the parking lot between my Daddy's grocery store and my Uncle Jake's gas station. I got the crushed ice and syrup from Uncle Jake and was paid a commission on sales. Traffic was good and my overhead was low. But like any other ten-year-old kid, I began to lose focus once the novelty of the business wore off. That is, until the Fourth of July came around, and my dad and uncle let me keep *all* the money that I took in.

Man, oh, man, did I work that day! I really hawked my goods hard. I gave everybody triple sized sno-cones for a dime. If they didn't have a dime, I'd take a nickel! When business got a little slow, I hired some kids to greet the people as they parked their cars and to run around my dad's store advertising my sno-cones. The kids got two cents for every sno-cone they sold, and I kept eight (or, in the case of the nickel sno-cones, they got one cent and I kept four). I made so much money on that Fourth of July that I bought everyone a load of candy and ice cream, tons of firecrackers and about a month's supply of BBs. I was a real high roller. I liked that feeling. No, I LOVED IT!!!!

• • •

NOT ONLY did my sno-cone and pencil business boom, but so did my dad's retail store. From the time it opened in 1946 until 1954, the Mack Henson Grocery & Market quadrupled in size and eventually included clothing, hardware, and jewelry departments.

Late in the summer of 1954, we held the famous three-day Mack Henson Grocery & Market 8th Anniversary Celebration. We replaced the sno-cone stand in the parking lot with a small Ferris wheel. One of the grocery wholesale companies that sold Aunt Jemima pancake mix sent out a real, honest-to-goodness Aunt Jemima look-a-like. Top Tobacco Company sent out the "World's Most Famous Champion Top Spinner," who just happened to live right in Abilene. Daddy made a deal to promote Tip Top fried fruit pies. We sold so many thousands of fruit pies (regular price: ten cents. Super introductory price: three for a dime) that the Tip Top company parked a truck full of fruit pies right in front of the store to replenish the stock. Wow!

Radio ads and word-of-mouth drew huge crowds to the celebration. Early every morning, my little brother Bennie and I dressed up like clowns—thanks to my Aunt Louise who made what I thought were real cool clown suits—and hitched up my donkey to a borrowed wagon. Then Old Man Hatfield, a family friend, and I drove all over town throwing candy to the kids, handing out flyers, and inviting everyone, young and old, to the 8th Anniversary Celebration. I remember it was so hot and humid that the grease paint on my clown face ran down all over, but it didn't bother me because I was having the time of my life. I was ten years old, a celebrity clown and making $3 a day!

I was totally exhausted by the end of each day, but I was so excited about the next day I could hardly sleep. When I did get to sleep, I dreamed about the day that I would have my own grocery store. "If only I could start now," I thought, "then I won't have to be bothered with going to school."

By the time I was ten, I knew for sure I wanted to be a trader. I guess my dad, Mack Henson, was really to blame. He, all three of his brothers, and his sister were independent business people and well respected. I had had a small taste of success myself, and when Daddy took the time to teach me some of his basic rules of business success, I was fascinated with his stories and his philosophy.

Mack believed in advertising and was quite a showman. Everybody in town knew who he was. He did a lot of community theater and really wanted to be a big time movie star, though he never did make it, thank goodness! He put his creative talent and his acting ability into his business. He sponsored a fifteen minute live TV show every Wednesday that was funny and silly and popular with everyone. He was a great master of ceremonies and hosted a lot of school and community functions.

On some Saturday mornings, he personally painted pictures of cartoon characters like Donald Duck and Mickey Mouse on our store windows. He didn't paint them quickly, but took his time—and drew a big crowd in the process. Kids, old people, everybody. Daddy explained that by standing outside and painting his window slowly, he advertised his business, provided free entertainment, and had a great chance to visit with his customers. He believed in building relationships with his customers and in being completely honest with them.

He told me never to loan my customers money. "If someone owes you $2 and doesn't have the money," he explained, "then they'll go to your competitor to buy their groceries because they'll be embarrassed to buy from you, and you'll miss out on them not buying $30 a week in groceries. So you're better off just giving them the $2 rather than loaning them the money."

I remember one hot day there was an elderly lady sitting in a car in our parking lot waiting for someone who was shopping in our store. Daddy gave her a sno-cone. I was upset about him giving away my merchandise until he explained that not only was it nice and respectful to give the lady a sno-cone, but after that she would probably become a loyal customer and tell her friends about our store. "It's good business to help people and be friendly," he said.

To me Daddy was a GENIUS!

Chapter Two

Texas Wheeler-dealer

"I didn't want to go to school. I wanted to keep working.
In my twelve-year-old mind,
I was already a successful businessman!"

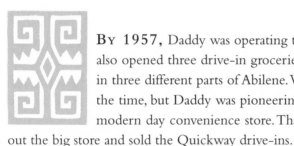 **BY 1957,** Daddy was operating the big store and had also opened three drive-in groceries, called Quickways, in three different parts of Abilene. We didn't realize it at the time, but Daddy was pioneering the concept of the modern day convenience store. That year Daddy leased out the big store and sold the Quickway drive-ins.

His older brother, Arthel, had gotten rich in a very short time developing land and building G.I. financed homes. Uncle Arthel had bought and moved to a big ranch south of Abilene, and we bought his "dream" house that he had built only a couple years before. I transferred from College Heights Elementary School to the newly built Fannin Elementary School. College Heights was about ninety-five percent Anglo and five percent Mexican-American but Fannin was about sixty percent Mexican-American. From the start, I loved Fannin because I knew a lot of the Mexican-American kids from our store and they all knew I was the son of "Mac-ken-soon" who was very popular and fair with his Mexican-American customers.

After my dad leased the store to a large chain outfit, I got out of the sno-cone business. But I was still on the lookout for a good trade. When I was in the 5th grade, I learned that if you wrote to the Texas Game and Fish Commission in Austin (now the Texas Department of Parks and Wildlife) they would send you beautiful eight and a half by eleven-inch color pictures of Texas wildlife with a story on the back. I wrote away several times for the pictures and each time I received about ten. Pretty soon I figured out that I could sell these beautiful color pictures for ten or fifteen cents each!

I started writing to the Commission every day. First I used my nick-name, Dusty, then my real name Richard, then my middle name Perry, then R.P. Then I started using made-up names using our home address. Soon all of the postage stamps around our house began to disappear. Business was real good for a while until I guess the Commission figured me out and stopped answering my letters. After that I got my friends and cousins to write, but once they got their hands on the pictures, they kept them for themselves!

Finally, one weekend I sat down and wrote to the game and fish com-mission of every state in the United States in care of their state capitol. No other state sent back pictures, but the mail did pour in! I was hooked! From that day on I've been fascinated with mail. There aren't too many things that excite me as much as getting out a huge mailing of new catalogs!

I WAS ALWAYS a second string football player and a C student. In all honesty, neither bothered me much because I really didn't have a passion for sports or studies and school was fairly easy. I was always a big talker and got along with everybody. The popular kids, the athletes, the nerds, and all the other groups in school accepted me. But it was the thugs who really fascinated me. They wore ducktail haircuts, black motorcycle jack-ets, and even carried their own cigarettes. I made friends with them. Most of them came from Sears Addition, a rough neighborhood near our school. Even though I was not a member of the group, I nevertheless came under their protection. Whenever I got into a fighting situation, I almost never blinked or backed down, but I always, always stalled for time until reinforcements arrived to rescue me.

IN THE SUMMERS, my family spent a lot of time at the lake house we had on Fort Phantom Lake near Abilene. My uncles, Arthel and Shorty, also had houses next to ours and everyone spent lots of time together, riding horses, shooting guns, playing poker, and, (my favorite) fishing.

I was always particularly close to and loved my Uncle A. J. "Shorty" Henson, his wife, Aunt Ann, and their kids. Uncle Shorty owned a construction company in Abilene for fifty years and there were a million Shorty stories. One time, he cut off three fingertips while operating a backhoe. After the accident, he pretty much convinced us kids that a donkey bit off his fingers.

Another time, his brother, Uncle Melvin, ran a trot line across the lake. Uncle Shorty decided to mess with him a little bit and hooked a rattlesnake on the end of the line. Boy, was Melvin surprised at his catch that day!

NOW, SOME PEOPLE sit back and relax with a fishing pole and daydream. NOT ME! While I was never particularly athletic or studious, I was a Little Boy Fisherman Deluxe! Besides helping my dad run trot lines from the boat, I was into big time freelance fishing on the side. To me it was all about numbers. The more hooks you had in the water the more fish you could catch. I grabbed every rod and reel and every cane pole I could find, baited them, and stuck them in the water. In addition I had every conceivable type of drop line, throw line, and net. I also waded out chest deep in the water to set my own mini trot lines.

I tested different size lines and hooks, some with corks and some bottom fishing. I experimented with every type of bait. Dough bait for carp, drum and buffalo. Blood bait—liver or shrimp—for catfish. Minnows for crappie, black bass and white bass. Worms for perch and bream. Some baits, like frogs and grasshoppers, were good for several types of fish.

I kept my bait fresh, checked it often, and changed it constantly when the fish weren't biting. I also kept my eye on the weather conditions, the time of day and the depth of my hook. I was ambitious when it came to fishing. I knew those fish were out there, and I couldn't wait to get at them. I would get up early, fish hard all day until late at night, and fall asleep exhausted.

I liked fishing because I could see the "payoff" immediately. I didn't give a damn about what kind of fish I caught or what size they were, just as long as they were on the end of my line. Fishing was my way of getting recognition because it was about the only thing I could do better than the rest of the kids. I loved the attention so much that sometimes I took fish off other people's lines and claimed that I had caught them. Even worse, I used to take the fish, tell my cousins that a fish broke their line, then rip off their hooks and sinkers. I would do almost anything to catch more fish than anyone!

IN THE SUMMER OF 1957, Daddy bought an old cement block ten-unit apartment house in a Mexican-American neighborhood just one block from the big store. I was brought into the project from the beginning and loved it. First off, Daddy hired some carpenters and painters to help fix it up. I'm not sure where he dug up these helpers, but I can say they were colorful. Daddy paid me forty cents an hour to hang around and make sure everything went smoothly and everyone stayed busy.

After the remodeling was done, we went all over Abilene looking for furniture and appliances at secondhand stores and garage sales. We furnished all the apartments, and I was very proud of our job. The next thing we had to do was rent the apartments at $10 a week or $35 a month. This was the part I loved most, because I got to be the guy who showed the apartments, took the money, and the tenants came to me with complaints, requests, etc. Our office was two blocks away, and I spent lots of time on my bicycle going back and forth. I remember how happy and sad I was when I rented the last apartment.

Happy because we had no vacancies, but sad because I had nothing left to sell. I liked the responsibility of being an apartment manager, and I liked hanging around with the Mexican-American families who rented the apartments. But most of all I liked being the one in charge at age twelve. I got along with my dad fabulously and we were both on the same frequency. We talked of doing more projects, but school was about to start again. I didn't want to go to school. I wanted to keep working. In my twelve-year-old mind, I was already a successful businessman!

THE NEXT SUMMER—the summer of 1958—we built a small strip center next to the big store with a barbershop, a beauty shop and Hawkeye's Diner. Daddy's big fishing buddy, six foot five inch Frank "Hawkeye" Span, was a house painter who had fallen on hard times because of a back injury. So they got together and opened up a blue-collar cafe. In trademark Mack Henson-style, we had a huge grand opening of Hawkeye's Diner on the Fourth of July, 1958. Regular size hamburgers were about twenty-five to thirty cents everywhere else. During our grand opening special, we sold a BIG hamburger with everything on it for ten cents. And boy, did we pack 'em in. People were lined up for about half a block waiting to grab a seat or place a to go order. One day alone we sold over 1,200 hamburgers. I was right in the middle of the fast and furious action. I loved it! Life was good.

The strip center also featured the newest business craze of the time: a coin-operated laundry. Maytag appliances were king. They owned the commercial market. We were one of the first "experimental" General Electric coin laundries. The GE washing machines weren't as commercially adapted as the Maytags, but GE was doing a lot of experimenting and improving their equipment. Daddy worked with the GE people and stayed loyal to them. They liked him a lot and offered to give him the financial backing to start putting GE machines in coin-operated laundries all over the United States. This was Daddy's chance to hit the real big time, beyond our wildest dreams!

In the winter of 1958-59 Mother and Daddy traveled a great deal scouting out locations for coin-operated laundries in Kentucky, south

Texas and Colorado. In January 1959, he chose his first three locations in the small Colorado towns of Alamosa, Monte Vista, and Del Norte, and was ready to start setting up the first of many planned GE coin-op laundries. Everything was set. Mother and Daddy were going to meet with the GE folks and sign their first deal on Monday morning.

On Sunday, the day before they were going to sign the deal, Mother and Daddy were driving on Wolf Creek Pass near South Fork, Colorado when they saw a "For Sale" sign on a ranch. The ranch was in the middle of the Rio Grande National Forest, with a big beautiful river running through it, huge pine trees, lakes, and two "postcard" looking log cabins. It was the most beautiful place my folks had ever seen.

Mother and Daddy never made it to that Monday morning meeting with the GE folks. Instead of laundry operators, our family became ranchers!

Chapter Three

Leaving Texas

*"Nope, it wasn't Texas, but it was home now
and all I could say was 'Let the adventure begin!'"*

 TEXAS WAS HOME and she had been good to us. As far as I know, none of my ancestors died in the Battle of the Alamo, which is the ultimate bragging right if you're a Texan, but our roots went deep and I had always been proud that all four of my grandparents were born in Texas in the 1800s. My granddad, C.J. Henson—or Old Man Henson, as he referred to himself—moved to Abilene in the early '40s from Seymore, Texas. He first worked as a produce peddler in Abilene and later owned a small neighborhood grocery store that became quite an institution. Aside from his grocery store, he traded in produce and junk, and built and sold cheap houses in North Abilene.

I remember my granddad as a heavy-set gentleman with white hair who wore suspenders, old-timey lace-up shoes, and an old hat. He liked to drive around in his old panel wagon, play dominoes, go fishing and talk about business, politics, his kids and grandkids. His domino-playing buddies were a hoot. I can still remember one of them who sold rat poison. To prove that his rat poison was safe for kids and animals, the old-timer would show off to people and eat some. I noticed that he let it dribble down his chin and never swallowed. Even as a school kid, I was impressed by the old man's con, though I didn't believe it for a minute.

Daddy had left Texas once before when he served in World War II. His unit had been ready to ship out for combat when he received news that Uncle Shorty and his family had been in a terrible auto-train wreck near Houston. Daddy got an emergency furlough to visit Uncle Shorty, who was in critical condition at the time, and by the time his furlough was up, his unit had shipped out. Daddy later learned that nearly his entire unit had been wiped out in combat.

Daddy was re-assigned to the Army Air Corps bombing range in Tonapah, Nevada where they trained bomber pilots. He and Mother rented a small storefront on Main Street in Tonapah. They opened the Quick Photo Shop in the front, and lived in a one room flat behind the store. This was wide open Nevada in 1945, so in between soldiering and processing photos, Daddy operated a few slot machines, did a little loan sharking and did a little trading in cars, motorcycles, nylons and other hard-to-obtain wartime luxuries.

He always said that if his family hadn't been in Texas, he would have stayed in Nevada. Now we were fixing to leave family and friends again. My folks had bought the ranch on Wolf Creek Pass. The house and apartments in Abilene had been sold.

Daddy had bought and traded for all kinds of things he needed for the Colorado adventure: jeeps, trucks, cement mixer, table saws, water pumps and a huge assortment of tools and equipment. Some of his Abilene employees were going to go with us, including Cleve Bilbry, a husky seventeen-year-old kid from down the street, and Jackie and Jeanie Woods, a young couple in their twenties. Uncle Melvin would be left in charge of our remaining properties which would, at least in theory, help bank-roll Daddy's ambitious new calling: Resort Owner!

Ten years after the California Gold Rush of 1849 came the Colorado Rocky Mountain Gold Rush of 1859. Folks back then were called '59ers. One hundred years later, the Henson family began their own rush to the

Colorado Rockies. By the time I had finished the eighth grade at North Junior High School, everything was a go!

After all the good-bye parties, the first group to leave was Mother, Daddy and my younger brother and sister, Bennie and Melba. They pulled a Jeep behind the family's 1955 Cadillac, and rushed to get to the ranch before the moving van. The next day, Jack and Jean Woods and their two little kids, Patty and Greg, set out in a Jeep station wagon pulling a trailer. Struggling along behind, with Cleve driving and me riding shotgun, was Daddy's 1952 Chevy pick-up, loaded down with a cement mixer in the bed, and towing another Jeep packed with equipment.

It was the most incredible trip I had ever been on. We had all kinds of mechanical troubles with the truck. We were hassled and shook down by police in New Mexico. We saw the Indians on the plaza in Santa Fe, and we barely made it up and over two mountain passes. The best thing about the trip was that we got to eat in restaurants and hamburger joints ALL THE WAY! Man, that was livin'!

Finally, we entered the San Luis Valley in Colorado and saw the part of the Rocky Mountains that would be our home. After we arrived at the ranch, I was impressed by the land, the horses and the log ranch house that was built in 1910. But I could tell right off that life on a ranch in Colorado was going to be a big change from life in Abilene, Texas! We had no TV and no telephone. The closest swimming pool was the hot springs of Pagosa Springs, some forty miles over the then dangerous Wolf Creek Pass. The friends and cousins I had grown up with were hundreds of miles away and I knew I was going to miss them.

The local people seemed to have a love/hate attitude towards Texans. Some were jealous and envious of us, while others were fascinated by us and admired our spirit. I remember how rough the Colorado people dressed and talked and how they drank beer openly. They had an accent that was very different than ours, and most of the local people had very little money.

Nope, it wasn't Texas, but it was home now and all I could say was "Let the adventure begin!"

Chapter Four

The Colorado Rancher

"You hook 'em, we cook 'em!"

 WE RENAMED THE RANCH Fun Valley, and while life was different, it was never dull. The first summer we built a cement miniature golf course. The locals were very confused by the strange foundations and forms we were pouring. We had a lot of fun telling them it was a brand new type of motel. After working on the cement crew, I knew right then and there that I would NEVER again be in construction, or any other business that involved manual labor!

Daddy realized early on that if he was going to own a successful fishing lodge and resort, he had to offer his customers good fishing. Tourists did not need a Colorado state fishing license to fish in our Class B Permit commercial fish pond and the Colorado Department of Parks and Wildlife stocked the rivers and non-commercial lakes on both the National Forest and on private land without charge. Daddy quickly became buddies with the local game warden and Fun Valley soon had the best fishing around.

The Colorado natives were avid fly-fishermen and looked down on bait fishing. But I didn't care. All I wanted to do was catch fish. Being an old hand at bait fishing back in Texas, I quickly adjusted my bait fishing skills to trout. I went off to my favorite fishing hole whenever I wanted and usually came back with a mess of fish in a short period of time. As far as I know, I was the only one who used trot lines for catching trout. That might have been because it was *illegal* to use trot lines in Colorado, but I never told anyone about my secret, and lucky for me, no one found out.

SOMEHOW I CAME TO BELIEVE that in Colorado you only had to go to school for eleven years. I was disappointed when I started ninth grade at Del Norte High School and got the official word: Colorado was just like Texas. Students had to go to school for twelve years.

Even though I never was much for school, in all honesty, I liked the Del Norte small school atmosphere. I was quite a novelty with my thick Texas accent and drew eager listeners to hear my tall tales. I played football that year and noticed that my teammates were scruffier than the athletes back home, and they all smoked. Serious athletes in Texas didn't do that, but what the hell, this wasn't Texas, so I lit up too. The coaches always tried to avoid seeing anyone smoke, so they wouldn't have to kick us off the team. That year we tied one game and lost all the rest.

THE WINTER OF 1959-60 was a doozie—lots of snow! We rode the school bus twenty-two miles to school every day, and every day I prayed that the school would be snowed out and closed, but it didn't happen very often. We cut holes in the ice and fished, and at night we listened to KOMA, a high powered radio station from Oklahoma City. That winter, Daddy was elected president of the South Fork Chamber of Commerce. He reorganized the Chamber and put together the first World Championship Raft Races down the Rio Grande from Creede to South Fork. The race was held the following June, when the water was highest. It became an annual event and is still held to this day.

•   •   •

IT MADE A BIG IMPRESSION on me just how poor the local people were. School closed for a while every year so that the students could go out and pick potatoes. Whole families of locals, Navajo Indians from the reservation in Arizona, just about everyone picked potatoes. Hunting season was an important time for everyone too. Folks didn't hunt for fun, they hunted for food. The game warden brought in fresh deer and elk road kill for the school cafeteria. The school lunches were twenty-two cents. Still, many kids were months behind in paying for their lunches, and the teachers refused to release their report cards until they paid up.

Even in our relatively affluent home, we were told to be more careful with money. We had spent a lot during the previous summer and needed every dime for construction of the planned motel and restaurant. This new financial conservatism was something I had never experienced before.

I had sensed in Abilene that a lot of people weren't as well off as we were, and I also knew that there were some people on the Southside who were rich beyond anything I could imagine. In fact, my cousin Andy and I often fantasized about making more money than we could spend, but as a child the difference hadn't been all that important to me. I never spent a whole lot of time thinking about status. My motivation for making money then had been mostly to be popular. I had tried to compensate for the fact that I wasn't particularly good at sports, or school, by being the one who always had money and could buy stuff for the other kids.

While it was an adventure to go to Colorado, it was also a time of personal turmoil for me. I was a young teenager and not exactly immune to the uncertainties and insecurities that went along with that, plus I was a long way from Texas and the safety of my friends and family. Now I was seeing, and understanding for the first time, what hard-core, grinding poverty was all about. I could see its effects all around me. I also realized, for the first time, that financial independence wasn't a given. I don't mind admitting that it scared me to realize that it was a whole lot easier to end up poor than rich!

I guess what happened to me was a "reality check" and it had a profound effect on me. My attitude toward money changed completely. Now I understood that money wasn't something to be taken for granted and that you needed it for more than popularity. Yeah, I still wanted to be a high roller, because I loved the feeling, but now my real, bottom line reason for making money became survival; not just "gettin'-by" survival, but survival on my terms: independent and comfortable. I was determined that someday I would have a successful business of my own.

IN THE SPRING OF 1960, we built a motel and a large restaurant at Fun Valley. That year I had made a deal with Daddy to let me run the new fishpond concession, or as we called it, the "pay pond." I couldn't wait. I was ready to make some M-O-N-E-Y!

My younger brother Bennie took care of the horse rides, while I took care of the fishing. My commercial fish pond was directly behind the restaurant. The fish truck from the commercial hatchery delivered fish anytime we ordered. Our cost was $1 per pound delivered live. The ideal length to buy was about ten inches. Trout that length weighed about a half a pound or less. We sold the fish to customers for ten cents an inch. We bought a lot of fish early in the season because by feeding them a lot (they loved Purina Trout Chow) we could grow them a couple of inches before they were caught.

I always hung around the back of the restaurant, where we had a nice patio and a bridge over the water. When people looked out the window or came out onto the patio, I'd throw some feed out. The water would turn black with fish, and they'd splash all over the place. I kept a small paper sack of fish food (always almost empty) and would give some feed to people and especially to little kids to throw out for themselves. Then I'd suggest they buy another sack of fish feed from the bartender. I had a pre-arranged hand signal with the bartender as to how much to charge for the sack—ten to fifty cents depending on what I judged they could pay. Sometimes I would get a bigger bag and offer it for $1. If they hesitated to buy the big bag, I always offered them the smaller bag. Feed was cheap, and the more you fed the fish the longer they grew. And all the time I tried to sell visitors on my "NO License Required, Guaranteed Catch Super Deal." I told folks that the fishing was good and cheap and that we'd cook the fish right in the restaurant. My slogan was, "You hook 'em, we cook 'em."

In my deal, I kept all the money we charged for cleaning (ten cents) and half of the money for the worms I dug and sold for bait, *plus tips!* As anyone in the hospitality business will tell you, getting tips is an art. At age fifteen, I became a hard-core hustler, part-time con artist, and master tip generator!

One of the things I did to get good tips was to check out the license plates of the cars that pulled into the ranch and pick my targets. The best tippers were from California, Oklahoma, Arizona, Texas and the Northeast. The worst were from Michigan, Minnesota, Wisconsin. And forget about the Coloradoans. I also ignored the folks we called "Two twos" (two kids with two cents) and looked for older people who were with grandkids. Grandparents with grandkids would pay almost anything you asked.

We fished with cane poles baited with worms or salmon eggs. I threw in the fish food. As soon as the trout hit the line, I popped the pole and set the hook. Then I let the customer bring in the fish. If they caught a lot of fish and didn't keep a close count, I always had some "add on" fish to add on to their catch.

I truly believe that everybody on earth has something they can do better than anyone else. Most people never ever know what their talent is, right? Well, my claim to fame then, and now, is cleaning trout. Yep. I can clean a trout in seven seconds flat! This is not a misprint. Our charge for cleaning fish was ten cents, but if the customer looked good, and caught six or seven fish, I would say in my sweetest voice, "I enjoyed helping you so much that I really don't want to charge you for cleaning your fish." This usually led to me getting a dollar or more as a tip!

Once in a while I miscalculated and some cheapo just said "Thank you" with no tip. In that case, I forgot all about Daddy's rules on how to treat your customers and went for revenge. I normally killed the fish by banging their heads on the side of the bucket. When you banged their heads, you could open up their gills with your thumb and with some practice, shoot a stream of blood wherever you aimed it. Sometimes, if I'd worked extra hard and gotten stiffed, my target was the face of the cheapo customer, or their white shirt or blouse. "Oh, excuse me," I'd apologize. "I'm soooo sorry." Other times, I'd just skim off one or two of their fish for the next "add on" and let it go at that.

IN ADDITION to my fish cleaning and worm business, I dug up and sold small pine trees, wild roses and wild raspberry plants. I also found that folks would buy pieces of wood that had been gnawed by beavers. I even sold a live chipmunk or two. If someone wanted to buy something, I did my best to find it and sell it to them. Not only did I love having a roll of walking-around money, I loved to make a good trade. And I still love it to this day.

Chapter Five

Valentine's Cakes
and a Pile of Dirty Laundry

*"When you're young and starting out
in business, sometimes you just don't know
where to draw the line."*

WE ONLY LIVED YEAR-ROUND in Colorado for two years. After that, we spent summers at Fun Valley and spent the school year in Abilene. My family has continued to do that since 1959.

I graduated from Cooper High School in Abilene, Texas in 1963, and then it was time for college. I knew I wasn't cut out for the books, but I went anyway to North Texas State University in Denton, Texas.

I lasted about a year and a half before I left. I had no use for college, and college had no use for me. The best thing about college was my roommate, Andy Henson, the son of my Uncle "Shorty" Henson. Andy was a couple of years older than me and was probably my most influential mentor, after my parents. Andy had a wild imagination and always dreamed of making millions. Now he is a multimillionaire.

Some of the other guys I met in college didn't turn out so well. My pledge brother in the Pi Kappa Alpha fraternity was Charles Watson. Charles was more or less an average wild fraternity guy when I knew him, but he later moved to California, hooked up with Charles Manson, and became known as Charles "Tex" Watson when he stood trial for the murders of Sharon Tate and the LaBianca family. He went to prison. I heard later that he turned to Jesus, became a minister and now lives with his wife and three kids in a mobile home on a California prison farm.

AFTER I LEFT COLLEGE, I moved back to Abilene for a while and started looking around for opportunities. I remembered how much I liked helping Daddy with his apartment complexes and so I figured I'd give real estate a try. I walked into a real estate office and met the owner, Don Sanderson. (That was not his real name, but the story is true.) He gave me an enthusiastic welcome.

"You wanna sell real estate? Great!"

"But don't I need a license or something?" I asked.

"Oh, don't worry about it," Sanderson winked. "We'll fix everything."

The phone rang, he told me to answer it, and I picked it up. I talked to a customer for a few minutes, hung up, shook hands with Sanderson and went home. Later that afternoon, Sanderson called me up. "Congratulations!" he boomed. "You just sold half a house." It was a split commission because it was my lead, but he sold the house. I didn't care about the split. I was in the real estate business. I wasn't even old enough to get my license, but that didn't bother Sanderson or anyone else in *that* office.

Old Sanderson was quite a character. The man would do absolutely anything to make a sale, and he had a lot of real estate to sell. This was during the cold war, and General Dynamics had set up a huge plant in Abilene to build nuclear missile silos. When the plant closed down in 1964 and 1965, the company moved out. Workers left with the company and abandoned whole neighborhoods. The FHA repossessed the homes. Sanderson was taking those repos and selling them as fast as we could, mostly to poor folks. We were selling three bedroom, one-and-a-half bath homes for $6,750. Nothing down, and a $100 deposit on the closing costs of $250. We would loan the buyers $75 for the deposit if they could come up with $25. Talk about a deal.

We used every trick in the book to sell those homes. Bait and switch newspaper ads. Hot box telephones. Sanderson was a great teacher and motivator and taught me a lot about closing the sale. "After you show 'em, just get 'em in the door and let me close 'em," Sanderson said.

One of the tricks he taught me was how to get customers back into the office after I'd shown them a house. When we got back into the office parking lot, instead of letting the clients drive away, I would grab a little kid and say, "Hey, come into the office and I'll buy you a Coke." The parents always followed the kid back into the office and BOOM, Sanderson and I would use heavy pressure to sell them a house before they knew what hit 'em. We called this "bouncing 'em off the wall." Back then I was young, hungry and had no scruples. Sanderson had even fewer.

SELLING REAL ESTATE just wasn't enough for me. I wanted to make big money fast. I had been fascinated by the mail ever since I sent off for wildlife photos as a kid. A buddy of mine and I came up with a great scheme. Abilene is a college town with three church colleges. My buddy Aaron Waldrop and I founded a group called the Young Christian Student Association. We were young, we were Christian and—according to Webster's dictionary—the definition of an association is two or more people having something in common. So we justified our association in that way.

Anyway, in February, we copied down the names and addresses of all the parents of the college students from the student directories and mailed them a letter. We offered to deliver a Valentine's cake on Valentine's Day to each student as a gift from their parents, and we asked for two dollars. That was a pretty good deal. You know, forty cents bought a lot of flour and sugar in 1965.

The Valentine's Day mailing drew a great response. We made $300 bucks a piece selling Valentine's Day cakes to the parents of those college kids.

• • •

AFTER THE VALENTINE'S DAY DEAL I was convinced that I was going to get rich. But there weren't enough holidays. So I thought and thought and I kept thinking that there had to be something else. Then it came to me: a "Who's Who" book for college students.

I was selling real estate, and all summer I worked on my letter. I made up an organization called Friends of Texas Students, and I named my publication *Spotlight On Campus*. I swear I can remember the pitch letter to this day, almost verbatim.

> *Dear Parents,*
>
> *Your son or daughter* (this was so crude you can't even believe it!) *has been selected to be introduced in Spotlight on Campus 1965. Whereas the standards of admittance are based on creditable lines of achievement such as leadership, athletic skill, scholarship, civil and organizational leadership… To help defray the costs of shipping, you will send $5 for your copy…*

While I was buying the envelopes at a wholesale paper company, I met one of their employees who was handicapped and in some type of club for handicapped people, so I hired the members of the club to address, stuff, and stamp envelopes. At the bottom of my pitch letter it said, *"Our thanks to the handicapped."*

The deal was appealing because if the kid was a good student, the parents wanted them to be in the book. And if the kid was a mediocre or poor student the parents wanted them to be included even more.

The response to *Spotlight on Campus* was like ninety-five percent. Orders just flooded in. Parents were sending pictures and writing samples and certificates—all kinds of stuff was coming in with the checks.

Man, I thought I had hit the jackpot! I bought a new Riviera, set up an office in my newly rented, fancy apartment with maps on the wall, and called friends to get student directories from all across the country. I even talked to Borden Duffel, our family CPA, about working for me full time. I was a twenty-one year old kid who knew he was gonna be rich, rich, rich.

Then one day the phone rang at the real estate office where I was working.

"Mr. Henson, this is the postal inspector. We'd like you to come down to the post office and speak with us…"

I went down to the postal inspector's office and sat down opposite the postal inspector and a U.S. Marshall. I was scared to death. The book wasn't even published. All I had done was collect the money.

The postal inspector said, "Mr. Henson, how did you select all these people to be in your book?"

I was too terrified to answer. But I knew that my letter said "selection was based on creditable achievement such as…"

They asked me again. "How did you select these people?"

I gulped. "Out of the student directory."

"Well," the inspector continued. "Which ones did you select for scholarship and which ones for…"

I leaned back and looked at the inspector. "You know, sir, I'm the kind of guy who believes that there is a little bit of good in everybody. And all of these people have some good in them…"

The inspector said, "OK, Mr. Henson, you are facing the possibility of federal mail fraud. We don't know if there is going to be an indictment…"

"Well," I said, "am I being charged?"

"We'll get back to you…"

A few weeks later, I got another call from the post office. "Mr. Henson, what are you doing on this book situation? Is it published?"

"I was going to ask you."

"What?"

"Well, I mean if you are going to indict me, then I was planning on using this money for my lawyer." I was shaking on the inside, but knew I had to keep calm.

"What about the people who have ordered books?"

"I'm not trying to cheat anybody. You're the guys who are stopping me from doing the service I have sold."

"We're not stopping you."

"Are you telling me that I'm under indictment and I can't produce the book?"

"No, we're not."

"Then what are you telling me?"

"We're telling you that there may be an indictment…"

"Fine. When I get inquiries about the books, I'm going to give them your name and have them call you." I realized that if they hadn't arrested me yet, I had some breathing room.

February was coming up, and I decided to try the Valentine's cake deal again. I talked with a banker in Abilene. He was a colorful character who had done all kind of crazy business deals. I somehow managed to meet him and he clearly liked me and my inventive ideas. He owned a bank in Abilene and a car dealership in Eastland, Texas. He once had two hundred white Oldsmobiles, and sold them as "two-tone" cars, offering to paint the top or bottom any color a customer wanted. He also started a pirate radio station on a ship twelve miles off the coast of Haiti and advertised tobacco and other things because he was outside the twelve-mile limit. I was fascinated with his stories, and he was kind of a mentor to me.

I described the Valentine's deal in Abilene, but I was careful not to mention the Who's Who deal and my problems with the postal inspectors. I told him that I wanted to do the Valentine cake deal again, but this time at the huge University of Texas in Austin. He agreed to finance the deal for fifty percent of the profit, and I sent out letters to the parents of all the students at the University of Texas. Same letters, same hand addressed envelopes.

This was my first big mail-out (over twenty thousand pieces), and it's hard to describe just how really exciting this was to me at the time. I guess I could say when I do a big mail-out, even to this day, the excitement is almost sexual. To me, when I make a large mail drop, it feels great. It's kind of like a huge ejaculation.

Some time after Valentine's Day, the banker gave me a call. "Dusty, I got a call from these postal inspectors and they want to see us…"

So we walk in there, and the banker was surprised when the inspectors knew me. The inspectors were even more surprised when they saw me walk in. When we got down to business, the postal inspector said that some of the cakes didn't get delivered down in Austin. The banker shook his head, "You mean I flew all the way over here to talk about some cakes that hadn't been delivered? Of course we'll refund the money."

I never did have to tell the banker about my earlier run-in with the postal inspector, as the authorities finally told me that they would not indict me unless I failed to deliver the book to the folks who had ordered it. So I published *Spotlight on Campus*.

Although I got out of the situation OK, my experience with the postal authorities scared the shit out of me. I changed forever after that experience. Since that time, I have always practiced and preached honesty— both in my business and in my personal life. No amount of money is worth the risk of going to jail. There are just too many ways of making a good living without having to break the law.

IN 1965, I joined the Texas National Guard Reserves. No one in my unit took their military training too seriously. One year we had a two-week summer training camp at Texas Tech University in Lubbock, Texas. The commanding officer gave us a speech and said that there were some things to work out—like laundry. Laundry. I did some quick math. There were 160 guys in this unit and each one needed a cleaned, pressed uniform every day. That was a lot of laundry and potentially a lot of money.

I went up to the CO and said, "Look, I'll take care of the laundry. I gotta guy that can do it." He said fine. Well, I didn't have anybody. I called James Richards, my cousin who was a student at Texas Tech, and I said, "Go find us somebody to do all this laundry. We got a chance here to make some good money."

Well, we found one old guy. I didn't like him much to start with, and we immediately started arguing about money and about how much he'd charge. Finally I said, "Look. We'll wash the stuff. All you do is just press it and we'll pay you for that."

So my cousin and I went to the laundromat. Man, we took up thirty machines. "Stuff those machines full," I told my cousin, "or we're gonna be here all night."

So we stuffed those old machines full of laundry. We had no idea what we were doing, but I'd already collected the money. And when the wash came out, it was awful. Big white soap stains all over everything. And this old guy who hated us anyway, I had already prepaid him. Well, that SOB just pressed up all the laundry, soap stains and all, and delivered it. Lucky for me, I blamed the guy who had done the pressing, and everyone thought it was a big joke.

In 1966, I went through basic training at Fort Bliss in El Paso. In 1968, I moved to El Paso and sold real estate for Paul Barry, but mostly I began to venture across the border into Mexico. I spent most of my time partying and chasing girls, just like any other young man. But I began to trade and to help run the family resort in Colorado in the summer season. Soon after that I had the opportunity to open my first trading post.

Chapter Six

The Old West Hotel

"I packed the place full of merchandise.
We sold everything—from candles to my cousin's pottery."

 MY FAMILY'S BUSINESS—Fun Valley Resort in South Fork, Colorado—has always been geared more toward the middle class family vacationers rather than the jet setters or the rich and famous. But we did get some famous guests through the years. Back in the mid-1960s, Texas Governor Preston Smith from Lubbock was a regular Fun Valley guest, before, during and after his term. He was a nice man and a good tipper who really liked fly-fishing.

Square dancing was always a major part of Fun Valley's entertainment and my dad knew square dance callers and square dances all over the country and especially in Texas. When Governor Smith was elected to his second term, Daddy suggested to the governor that he host the first ever Square Dance Inaugural Ball in Austin. The idea caught on, and the location had to be changed several times as the guest list swelled. Daddy had my mother send a letter to President Johnson inviting him to the dance. And I'll be damned, one morning the PRESIDENT OF THE UNITED

STATES called Mack Henson and apologized for being unable to attend the function.

As you might expect, the first ever Governor's Inaugural Square Dance, in 1966, was a huge success and about 1,500 attended. Daddy was the master of ceremonies, mother was the official greeter, and Fun Valley brochures and summer square dance schedules were everywhere. When the Governor's entourage entered, Daddy asked the crowd to please make way, and the crowd parted like the Red Sea parting for the Israelites. Governor Smith stepped up to the microphone, made a short speech and thanked everyone for coming to the 1966 first ever Texas Square Dance Inaugural Ball.

TWENTY MILES from Fun Valley is the town of Del Norte. It's not a resort town. It's a typical small Colorado town located in the San Luis Valley in the foothills of the Rocky Mountains. Right in the middle of town stood an old hotel. It was a typical small town hotel with rooms upstairs, and stores on the ground floor. For some reason, Daddy bought the place in 1969. He paid $19,000 for it, $3,000 down. That same year, he bought the Spruce Ski Lodge in South Fork for my brother Bennie to manage.

I managed the hotel and began splitting my time between El Paso and Colorado. The hotel wasn't run down. It was just old, built in 1872. The previous owner had half of the stores on the first floor rented. The first thing we did was to say, "We're gonna need this space back. We'll help you get a new place, but we're gonna need this space." Of course there wasn't a written contract anywhere. So we took over all the stores on both sides of the building and put the hotel office right on the corner of the block.

We built an old-timey boardwalk around the front of the building, and a balcony around the second floor. You had to climb out of the window to get to the balcony, but that was OK. We built a fountain in the back courtyard, and we painted gunfighters on the wall. James Richards, my cousin, even made a big cowboy head that we put on the corner of the building.

We tore down all the walls between the stores on each side to make one big store. After we gutted those stores we set up a kind of Wild West shopping mall with all kinds of crafts shops and curio shops. James Richards had graduated from Texas Tech and set up a pottery shop. I had a leather store, a Mexico import shop, and a cowboy and Indian store. We had a cowboy artist in the store for two years. That was back in the old hippie times, although I never considered myself a hippie because I was too interested in making money. But we did have a candle shop.

I MANAGED THE OLD WEST HOTEL in the summertime. We had thirty-two rooms, most had private baths, some had adjoining baths and a few of them, like old room Number 9, had neither. The bath was down the hall European style. I liked to be the one renting the rooms, especially when the whole town was gettin' full. I never did really take advantage of people, but I did like getting the higher prices.

One time a guy came in and asked, "Gotta room?"

"Yessir," I said, "I got a nice room for $18."

"Hmmm…eighteen bucks. I don't think so. I guess I'll just go sleep in my truck."

"Now hold on," I said. I carefully studied my guest book. "OK," I said. "Here's a pretty nice room for $15."

"Oh, that's a little high," he said. "I guess I'll just go on down the road."

"Well," I sighed. "I do have one room. I've been meaning to paint it but I haven't got around to it yet…"

The fellow looked interested. "How much is that room?"

"I'll let you have it for twelve bucks."

"OK, I'll take it."

I was selling the same room all along. It was the last room in the hotel, old Number 9.

• • •

SOMETIMES, things were pretty slow at the hotel, especially in the winter. Sitting around the lobby in the winter of '69 my cousin James and I were reading the *Denver Post* when I noticed an article about how the Boston Strangler—Albert DeSalva—was making jewelry in jail. It was hippie times, you know, and everything was all anti-establishment. I got to thinking and I said to my cousin, "What if we get the Boston Strangler to make us a casting of a choker with little hands around the neck? I bet we could sell the hell out of a choker made by the Boston Strangler."

We laughed about the idea. Then I actually sent a letter off to Albert DeSalva. I didn't say anything about the choker in the letter. I just said that I'd read the article and wondered if he would be interested in making some jewelry for us.

A couple of weeks later, I got an answer in the mail. I was real excited, you know, and nervous. I opened the letter and started reading. And the first line of the letter read, "Mr. Henson, Your letter chilled me..."

Imagine, my letter chilled the Boston Strangler!

Well, the reason that it chilled him didn't have anything to do with the jewelry idea. It was because his stepdaughter lived in Colorado. But I've always liked the fact that my letter chilled the Boston Strangler. We never did get it together to make the chokers, because somebody killed him in prison.

AS THE '60S CAME TO A CLOSE, I was out of the Army and itching to go out and take on the world! I spent more and more time in Mexico, and I decided that I wanted to make my living importing and selling Mexican curios and jewelry.

"Poor Mexico, poor Mexico...so far from God, but so close to the United States...."
—PORFIRIO DIAZ, 1910

In those early years, I fell in love with Mexico and with doing business in Mexico. Mexico business can either be the best, most fun time you've ever had or an absolute nightmare. It's usually a little bit of both. I love Mexico and the Mexican people with all my heart, but you always must remember that this is a very different country and can test your patience. It's a different way of business. It's a different culture.

The first thing I learned about trading in Mexico was that I'd better learn to speak Spanish. There is no substitute for knowing the language. I learned early on that because folks don't speak English doesn't mean they are dumb. And even if they act a little bit slow, it could well be just an act. I took some classes and taught myself and continued teaching myself for the next thirty years.

THE FIRST MISTAKE traders make in Mexico is being haughty or giving the impression that they are superior. It's that old thing about "Big Brother United States." You can't go into Mexico thinking like a big-shot American or you're going to have problems real quick.

I learned that the worst thing to do in Mexico was to make comparisons. Every culture is different, and when you are doing business in another country, you must respect their culture. Especially in Mexico, it is important to be very polite and show genuine respect for their culture, family and country. I learned quickly to be careful when making jokes or saying anything that might be taken wrong.

Basically what I learned as a young man trading in Mexico can be summed up as follows:

- Don't take advantage of people.
- Don't beat them down on price too much.
- But don't let them retire off you.
- Keep your people coming back.
- Never apologize for making money.

Even though I worked pretty hard, sharpened my skills at selling, learned Spanish and had the basic desire and ambition to be independent, I was not very successful. I was single and not well disciplined at all. You know, spending way too much time drinking, doping, after-hours gambling and getting well acquainted with all the bars and "whatever" joints in infamous Juárez, Mexico.

• • •

EVEN WHILE I was running the hotel and trading goods from Mexico, I couldn't help but come up with other money-making schemes. My favorite was "The Truth About Mexican Dentures."

It was an information business. I put a classified ad in the small-town newspapers within a couple of hundred miles of El Paso. I also ran classified ads in *Field and Stream, Senior Living* and other publications that were popular with older retired folks. The ad read something like this, "Mexican Dentures...$70 for upper and lower plates...For more information send name, address and $1 to The Truth About Mexican Dentures, P.O. Box 12360, El Paso, Texas."

When someone sent me a dollar, I sent them a list of denture clinics and prices in Juárez, and some general information about how to get there, where to stay and where to eat. The business never was hugely successful, but it drew a steady stream of dollar bills. Years later, I still got letters every once in a while, asking for The Truth About Mexican Dentures.

THE OLD WEST HOTEL quickly became one of the biggest tourist attractions in southern Colorado. One of the best experiences I had at the hotel was when a blonde haired, hazel-eyed young lady walked in with a proposition I couldn't refuse.

PART 2
The Business Partnership

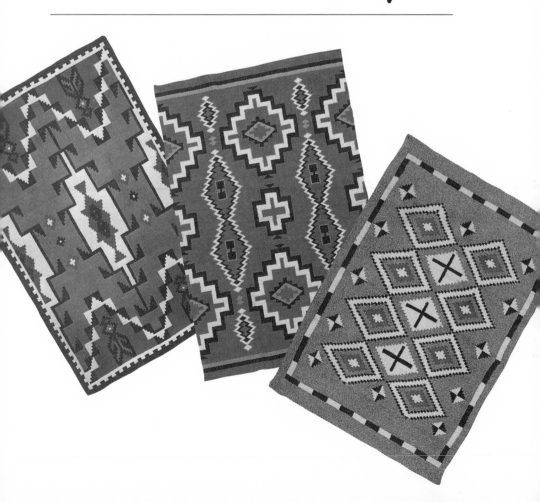

Chapter Seven

Tying the Knot

*"Life with Dusty hasn't always been easy,
but I guarantee you, it's never been dull,"*

—BONNIE HENSON

 THE GOOD-LOOKING WOMAN who came into the
Old West Hotel in the summer of 1974 was a school-
teacher from Iowa. She was doing advertising work for a
development in Pagosa Springs, which was just across
Wolf Creek Pass from the Old West Hotel. Bonnie came
into the hotel and asked me if I'd let her put cards advertising the Pagosa real estate development in every hotel room. The deal
was that if someone went to listen to their pitch, they'd get a free round
of golf, or a camera or some other prize. I was hesitant until Bonnie
explained that she would give me $75 up-front to put the cards in the
hotel, and $75 for each hotel customer that made a purchase. It was a deal
I couldn't refuse. Little did Bonnie or I realize that it would be the first of
thousands of deals we would work together as man and wife and founders
of El Paso Saddleblanket Company.

Bonnie can probably tell you best in her own words about how her
life changed when we got together. *"Some people daydream about escaping
their day-to-day routines and running away with the circus. I didn't need this*

fantasy—from the time I met Dusty Henson, life became a three-ring event. Having been a somewhat introverted elementary school teacher, my life took an irreversible turn when I took up with a wild and crazy gypsy trader.

"Seeing the Old West Hotel for the first time gave me some insight into the business personality of a twenty-nine-year-old bachelor named Dusty Henson. I thought the billboard down the road probably exaggerated when it boasted 'Over 100,000 Items.' Well, that turned out to be a modest understatement. The shops were packed with merchandise, floor to ceiling. Every conceivable inch of wall space or support column was plastered with Old West memorabilia. There were even items hanging from the ceiling.

"Everything was so accessible, so inviting. I am sure every kid blew his entire vacation allowance at the Old West Hotel. This was the absolute, ultimate tourist trap. Most everything was reasonably priced and "3 for $5" and "5 for $7.50" signs encouraged quantity purchases. My old desire to be in marketing rekindled, and I was eager to get to know the mind behind this operation."

BONNIE FINISHED UP her business with the development company in the fall of 1974. Or the business finished with her. At any rate, she was out of work, and I was ready to hit the road. I asked Bonnie, "I'm going to Mexico. Would you like to come along?"

Bonnie said, "Sure." It was an easy decision. A new owner had just bought the real estate company she was working for and had fired everyone. She didn't have a job, so she didn't have anything to lose. Mexico sounded great.

That was in 1974, and we've been together ever since. For us, marriage has meant much more than a honeymoon. It's meant building a life together, and we have built a life together through our business.

BONNIE'S CHILDHOOD was a lot different than mine. I'll let her tell her story for herself.

"About the same age that Dusty was wheeling and dealing sno-cones, I was helping a neighbor lady sell Tupperware in a small town in Iowa. My role in the

Tupperware party was two-fold. First, I demonstrated how to make homemade popsicles using the Tupperware freezer set and explained the savings over the store-bought kind. Then I demonstrated the special technique of closing the food storage containers so as to make them air-tight.

"The thrill of the sale did not capture me as it did Dusty. I just hoped my future career would be something more challenging than showing people how to burp their Tupperware."

Bonnie went from burping Tupperware to flipping hamburgers.

"While working at Dalton's Dairy Queen in Glenwood, Iowa, I overheard the owners debating whether or not they could survive the hamburger wars. The competition was selling hamburgers six for a dollar. I suggested that rather than arguing, they should sit down and put a pencil to the problem. 'How?' they asked. The next day I charted out the cost for one unit item (meat, bun, condiments, overhead, etc.) It was a close call, but we figured that if we could sell a sundae, or at least of couple of ice cream cones, with each hamburger purchase it would work. The sale began. It was a success. I was offered the position of assistant manager but I had just been accepted to the University of Iowa and off I went.

"Direct sales didn't interest me, although advertising and marketing did. As hard as I tried to pursue that major, I failed—not so much academically as socially. In the 1960s the MBA program was very much a fraternity. So I got a degree in elementary education and became a school teacher for a few years. Then I went to Colorado, got a real estate license, met Dusty, and we headed to Mexico."

ON MY THIRTIETH BIRTHDAY, September 26, 1974, we packed up my Chevy Impala and left Colorado for Mexico. We headed to San Miguel de Allende where we met a fellow, and I started dealing a bunch of his jewelry. After that, we went to Querétaro, one hundred miles north of Mexico City, where we bought some turquoise and a bunch of opal, mostly fire opals. I was convinced that fire opal was the next thing. We took the opals to Guadalajara to have them set in silver. It was a good trip, and we found some great antiques and Spanish colonial religious paintings to market along with the Mexican jewelry. While I was busy making deals, Bonnie was having her first experiences as an international traveler.

"When we first arrived in Mexico, my ability to speak Spanish was not much more than 'dos tacos por favor.' I knew at least that I wouldn't starve. But a dilemma arose when I ran out of clean clothes. I took Dusty with me to the hotel desk and had him ask in Spanish, 'Where do people go to wash their clothes?' Dusty got an answer and we started walking. After following the directions 'tres cuadros y vuelta a la izquierda' (three blocks, turn left), we found to our surprise not a laundromat, but the river where a dozen women were cheerfully pounding their laundry on the rocks. Sometimes, even when you understand the words the answer isn't quite what you expect."

WE TOOK THE MERCHANDISE we bought in Mexico and began traveling back and forth from our home base in El Paso to sell our goods in New Mexico, Arizona and southern Colorado. We began to meet a lot of good folks who had saddle shops, tourist curio stores and Indian trading posts. We sold our jewelry and other products and lived the life of gypsy traders. It was a cash only business, and we made lots of cash. Bonnie was shocked at first by the change in her lifestyle.

"As a young woman, I never could have imagined the fast paced life of a trader travelling to the far ends of the earth. When Dusty started El Paso Saddleblanket Company, it was little more than a one-horse operation. Well, let's say one-pick-up truck operation. Though the hours were long, it was a great lifestyle with no phone and no boss to answer to."

The main challenge Bonnie and I faced as a team was learning how to trust one another. I had to learn how to trust Bonnie's quiet, analytical perspective on problems. She had to learn how to trust my West Texas instincts. Slowly, we learned how to work together: a semi-outlaw border trader and a quiet midwestern schoolteacher.

"When we got together, my life took a very unusual turn. All my strict daily routine, conscientious budgeting, and well-organized plans were turned upside down as we gypsied through Mexico and the Indian Reservations of the Southwest.

"Finally, when I started to grasp what trading was all about, I realized that I could learn a lot about advertising and marketing from Dusty and that he could use some of my organizational skills. Thus, out of chaos came a great union.

Not only a business partnership but a marriage.

"In business Dusty is the runaway locomotive full of ideas and enthusiasm. He often complains that I am the brakeman. What most would call a train wreck is actually a finely-tuned, well-maintained business machine that operates out of cooperation and endless discussion.

"My family was a little concerned when I quit teaching and took off with Dusty. It's not that trading was foreign to them. In fact, my father's father was quite a wheeler-dealer in the early 1900s. They owned a huge farming operation, the local grain elevator, and the stock yards in a small, southwest Iowa town. Five children out of eight went off to college in high fashion wearing coonskin coats and driving their own Model T Fords. Unfortunately, the Depression wiped out all their holdings in 1929-1933. Some of my conservatism stems from this family experience."

BONNIE AND I had fun buying and selling all kinds of things, until we found the one product on which we could build a steady, on-going business. That product was the Mexican, handwoven, Southwest-style rug.

Chapter Eight

The New Navajo Rug

"I'm a trader not a collector."

 **WE WERE MOSTLY** still focusing on jewelry when we stumbled into something that would change our business forever. It was just a routine trip across the river to restock some silver from a wholesaler named Mauricio in Juárez.

Mauricio was a classic border character. He was a Jewish trader whose family had emigrated from Poland to Mexico. Mauricio was into a little bit of everything. He liked to sit at the front of his shop next to an ice chest, filled with soda for kids, and beer for adults. He spoke English in a deep, husky voice with a thick Polish/Spanish accent.

"Dusty," he growled when he saw me. "Dusty, come in. I have something for you."

Well, I'd gotten to know Mauricio back when I ran the Old West Hotel. I'd bought some jewelry from him and his brother, Julio. But when I went down to visit him this time, Mauricio had a new item he wanted me to see. "Dusty," he said. "Look at these blankets my brother Julio's making."

I studied them carefully. They were more tightly woven and more intricate than the old Casa Zia saddleblankets I had been selling for years.

These were a new style of rugs and saddleblankets with designs revived from old Navajo rugs. Julio had even put out a brochure. The photo on the cover of the brochure was completely fake (some Native American weavers standing at an old, vertical loom), and some of the color combinations were hideous. But the saddleblankets and rugs were sturdy and affordable. "You can sell a lot of these," Mauricio said. We thought so too. We could see the potential and we figured the small details could be worked out later.

He was right. Today, we are still selling saddleblankets and rugs that have designs very similar to the ones I first saw more than thirty-five years ago.

WE STARTED OUT selling our new products out of our pick-up to Indian traders, and pawn shops on the reservations: the clients we had gotten to know in the jewelry business. The Indian trading posts were owned by several families, like the Tanners (an old Mormon family) and the Ortegas.

One of the trading post operators we met was Maxie Ortega of St. Joseph, Arizona on Route 66, just west of Gallup, New Mexico. Maxie had been trading Navajo rugs for decades, and took a close look at our Mexican made saddleblankets and rugs. Maxie liked what he saw, but he had a lot of suggestions. He told us which colors to use for which rugs. He showed us how to make the corners flat and which rugs needed a border and which rugs didn't need a border. He told us about the Spirit Line, the Tree of Life and other traditional designs. Maxie was the one who really helped us take the Mexican-made saddleblankets and rugs and redesign them for the American consumer market. We were so pleased with his suggestions and his enthusiasm that we always stopped to see him, giving him first pick of every new load of merchandise.

IN THE SUMMER MONTHS we focused more on New Mexico. All winter we had coached the Mexican weavers on colors and designs that we thought would go over well in Albuquerque and Santa Fe.

One Friday, we headed across the border, picked up the rugs, finished the necessary documentation, and crossed the rugs through customs into El Paso. Then we took off up the highway and arrived at Santa Fe in the wee hours of the morning.

We had run a small classified ad in the *New Mexican*, a Santa Fe newspaper and sent out some very simple post cards inviting the tourist shop, western store and trading post owners to see our "new" weavings at the Ramada Inn on Cerrillos Road in Santa Fe starting at noon on Saturday.

We got up, put the mattress up against the wall, unloaded our rugs and blankets, and set up a display in our hotel room.

Then we waited. And waited. It was so slow that we even sold a family of tourists from New Jersey or somewhere a couple of rugs. Then one guy showed up and bought a very small order. Then one other guy called, asked a couple of questions and said he might get back later. THAT WAS IT. A HUGE DISAPPOINTMENT!!!

On the way back to El Paso, we sold some stuff to some Santo Domingo Indians at their pueblo and sold some more rugs in Old Town Albuquerque to Manny Goodman at the Covered Wagon Trading Post on the plaza. Despite our disappointment, Bonnie and I talked things over and decided to give Santa Fe one more shot the following Saturday.

The next Friday there was a long line at the international bridge and the customs agents were not too speedy. Finally, we cleared customs, then took off on the long six-hour drive to Santa Fe. We damn near flipped the load dodging a coyote at Truth or Consequences, New Mexico. Anyway, as we were checking into the Ramada Inn, the night clerk said, "Are you the folks with those Meskin' rugs?"

"Yeah, why?"

"Hey, the phone has been ringing off the wall for you."

"OK, OK. Good Night…," I said.

8 A.M. Saturday. Bang! Bang! At the door our first customer with a $600 sale. Not bad, considering the show didn't open until noon. 11 A.M.—another customer and another pretty good sale. Noon—five or six more customers showed up, and they kept showing up all day long. By the end of the day we'd sold out, but I was still giving out my just-printed business

cards and TRYING to act calm and cool! We sold out EVERYTHING! Even some odd lot Taxco silver jewelry and a couple Mexican saddles were gone.

It was amazing. The first weekend, nothing. The second weekend a sellout. We didn't know what caused our good fortune, but we didn't care. We had introduced a product that we truly believed in, and it was a great seller.

We later found out that the week after our first Santa Fe show, the owner of New Mexico's "premier snob gallery" wrote this long "do-gooder" letter to the editor of the *New Mexican* warning store owners and everyone about these "new" rugs from Mexico which were made so well that they compared to the authentic high-priced Navajo rugs. The gallery owner was trying to stop people from buying our rugs, but, in-stead, gave our product some of the best publicity it had ever had. I felt so indebted to the guy that I mailed him an anonymous Christmas card that year that included a crisp hundred dollar bill. He later found out who sent the Christmas card and, in the end, we all had a good laugh over it. Later, I even called on him to try and sell him some rugs. He never bought any, but we became pretty good friends through the years.

I HAVE ALWAYS BEEN FASCINATED by the history of handwoven textiles. Nomads in the Middle East started handweaving more than a thousand years ago, and the craft has almost always been a commercial endeavor. Thus, there is little recorded as to the origin of designs. Generally, traders have greatly influenced the patterns, color, and quality control of the world's handweaving. From the earliest experimentation with lines and angles, weavers have continually adapted and absorbed ideas from other cultures to upgrade the craft and increase the marketability of their handwoven product.

In the New World, between 1800 and 1900, Navajo Indians learned handweaving techniques from the Spanish and the Pueblo Indians. Until the late 1800s, the products the Navajos made were simple blankets for wearing and Chief's blankets that were traded to the Plains Indians. What people think of as Navajo-design rugs were designed mostly by early territorial traders using ideas from photographs of Persian carpets mixed with Pre-Columbian architectural designs from the Mitla ruins in Mexico. By combining these design features with sheep's wool, imported dyes, and some entrepreneurial spirit, Navajo weavers began to produce a marketable product. Today, the finest Navajo rugs are extremely expensive.

As traders, we continue to perform an important role in the evolution of handweaving. We are constantly working to create handwoven items of quality, economy, and above all, something the consumer feels good about acquiring. We continue to reintroduce popular old patterns in exciting new design combinations, new sizes and new colors.

Some folks have criticized us by saying that our Navajo-style hand weavings are not traditional enough. These folks don't know what they're talking about. For one thing, we have always, always been proud to say that the weavings we sell are produced in Mexico. For another thing, the manufacture of hand weavings has always depended on market demand as interpreted by traders. This has been true throughout history, and it is still true today. So, if customers demand hunter green, burgundy or cream colors, we are always willing to bend the rules of traditional red, black and white, and give them what they want. For nearly forty years, El Paso Saddleblanket has proudly specialized in quality handweaving mostly from Indians in Mexico. For some products, we have contracted the artistic skills of weavers in Guatemala, Ecuador and India.

I'm not a collector. I'm a trader. I've always been more concerned about something selling than being authentic. It's like cars. Some collectors will say, that's got a twelve volt battery, the real ones only have six. The first thing I do when I get an old car is to put in a twelve volt battery. The same is true with the Indian rugs and saddleblankets. If I think a traditional rug design will sell better if the red is a little brighter, I'll make it brighter. Most customers want quality and good-looking design. They don't care about strict authenticity. Certainly most Native Americans don't care. Some of our biggest clients now are the Indian casinos. They want merchandise that moves.

We will continue to modify our designs and contract with skilled weavers from around the world to respond to market changes and to bring our customers the highest quality Southwestern-style hand weavings at the lowest possible price. That has been the philosophy behind handweaving since the dawn of civilization, and it continues to be our philosophy at El Paso Saddleblanket.

Chapter Nine

Guatemala

"In some weaving areas, I had whole villages in remote Guatemala, entire towns, working. I take a lot of pride in that fact, not that anybody would be starving without El Paso Saddleblanket Company, but I think that some people are eating and living a little bit better."

JUST WHEN OUR BUSINESS was really taking off, we hit a snag. We couldn't get our beautiful new rugs out of Mexico. The administration of Mexican President Escheveria was decidedly anti-American and anti-trade. Importing from Mexico became almost impossible. Just when we had discovered the perfect product, our source was cut off. We had to find new weavers in a new country as fast as possible. That country was Guatemala.

Traveling has always been a major part of what it takes to run El Paso Saddleblanket Company. But the year we spent in Guatemala—from January to December, 1977—was the longest time we lived continuously outside of the U.S. Years later, Bonnie wrote down the story of our Guatemala experience. It was a pretty wild time.

"Visiting Guatemala for the first time in 1976 was not a pleasure trip securely planned and packaged by Grayline Tours. We were on a mission of grave financial interest. Because it had become so very difficult to do business in Mexico

under the rule of President Escheveria, we were searching for a country to move to for the purpose of entirely relocating our weaving operation. We knew that Guatemala had weavers. What we didn't realize at first was how far out in the boondocks and up in the mountains the skilled artisans lived.

"It was necessary to carry small change of the local currency. Going to a bank to cash some traveler's checks was not quite as easy as you would have thought. The lobby was full of people standing in slow-moving lines. Every transaction was done with a manual adding machine (not electric... the big old clunky kind) and before any money changed hands it took the rubber stamp of three or four people.

"Finally reaching a teller, we were told we were in the wrong line. Somewhat frustrated, but without profanity, we silently threw up our hands in useless anger, knowing the only thing we could do was go to the other line and wait again. But as I gestured, I also lifted my eyes to something I hadn't noticed before. I nearly fainted dead away when I saw on the mezzanine above no less than ten soldiers pointing AK-47s at the bank lobby.

"Dusty had to prop me up and calm me down. It took me a while to understand that the soldiers were there for our benefit... that Guatemala was under military rule, and unsurprisingly, they never have bank robberies.

"Even though the presence of armed soldiers throughout the city disturbed me, I learned later to accept the rationale. We learned to use the military for protection of our house, our business, and in our payroll trips to the Indian villages high in the mountains."

GOING FROM EL PASO, TEXAS TO GUATEMALA doesn't look so impossible in an atlas. It was just a matter of going from point A to point B. Right? We thought making the decision to go was the hard part. Wrong! The fun and futility had only just begun. Being young and in love and still somewhat naive, we boldly pushed onward. We liquidated our inventory, and sold off our truck and travel trailer, to raise as much capital as possible. Bonnie tells the rest of the story.

"Not everything in our inventory sold for cash. We ended-up taking about $50,000 worth of trade items. Some of this was components to make Indian jewelry and the rest was a starting inventory and franchise rights to the Argenion

water purifier business for Central America. The weaving business turned out to be only one of a dozen or more things we would get involved in during our stay in Guatemala.

BONNIE STILL HAD some serious reservations about moving to Guatemala. I knew she was concerned about our personal safety, as well as the loneliness of being an expatriate. So I promised to buy her a German shepherd puppy. As Bonnie wrote, she was thrilled with the idea.

"December 1976, Phoenix, Arizona. We were in the Michigan Trailer Park reading the classified ads in the newspaper. An ad jumps out at me: 'XTRA LARGE German shepherd puppies for sale.' That sounded like just what I needed as my protector for our foreign travels. That day we brought home this massive ball of fur and paws, only eight weeks old but all I could carry. We named him Sid.

"Just days later, we completed selling off all our extra stuff and headed for Guatemala in a Ford Econoline van. We left the trailer park just in time because we were about to get kicked out. It seems Sid had been leaving his doodoo on the neighbor's marigolds. In Arizona, in old folks' trailer parks, they don't permit children, pets or any disruptive behavior. Disruptive or not, Sid became part of our family. Even though Sid is no longer with us, German shepherds are still very much a part of our family. In fact, we now have four of them. But more dog stories later."

BEFORE WE LEFT THE UNITED STATES, we drove through Abilene, Texas, to say good-bye to my family. Randy Bruner, my brother-in-law, helped customize our Ford van so that we could hide some items that might be a problem going through customs inspections. A false bottom of a bunk bed became the hiding place for all the liquid silver jewelry components. I thought it was a pretty good set up, but, as Bonnie explains, it wasn't all that good.

"Everything rode very well until we were three days into Mexico. A junky old truck had a tire blowout right in front of us and Dusty had to hit the brakes

HARD and brought the van to a screeching, swerving stop. Everything from the back of the van crashed forward, filling the small open space reserved for Sid. Thank God Sid was OK. But in the crashing stop some of the packages of silver had broken. The van looked like some kind of cheap Christmas ornament. We had little bits of silver everywhere. It was impossible to clean it all up, and the next morning we had to cross over the border into Guatemala.

"When we pulled into the inspection station the guards were not friendly. They had been humiliated because, when they threw back the van's side door, they were terrified of little old Sid. I was told to take the dog 'over there' and stay out of the way.

"I got very nervous that the inspectors would confiscate our television and all our electrical appliances. Dusty started speaking Spanish to them and distributed all the beer we had left in the cooler. After completing their inspection they still had not found anything to get 'mordida'—literally a bite, a bribe—so they claimed we needed another permit to transport the dog into the country. $20, a rubber stamp, and a sigh of relief later, we were on the last leg of the trip into Guatemala City."

VERY SOON, we rented a house that came with two Indian maids from the mountains. We set up business, hired employees, and were producing all kinds of products for export. I always like to move forward quickly and decisively.

We traveled into the mountains to set up our weaving operations. It really forced us to improve our Spanish even though the textile weavers in the highlands spoke mostly Mayan Indian dialects. Spanish was their second language, but somehow we managed.

I brought some samples up to the village of San Francisco el Alto and spoke with the weavers there. We agreed on the price, and they agreed to have two hundred rugs ready on a certain date. I was back in the saddleblanket business and man, was I thrilled!

I called up Maxie Ortega and all my clients in the U.S. and said, "Hey, I've got good production down in Guatemala." And I sent them pictures and received a stack of orders. When the time came to pick up the order, I headed back up to the village, cash in hand, escorted by two soldiers with AK-47s. I asked where my rugs were and they pointed to a small pile. Instead of the two hundred rugs I was expecting, the weavers had produced only nine. My heart sank. The weavers explained that they had been planting corn, celebrating holidays and doing other things. I was shocked to learn that their priorities were so different from mine. What could have been a lucrative business, and would have been, turned out to be a bust.

I SAID TO MYSELF, "OK, if weaving blankets isn't our mainstay, let's move on to Plan B." Only problem was, we didn't have a Plan B. But we immediately went into an almost frantic production of other things that were more in our control, as Bonnie recalls.

"Everyday our dining room was filled with young ladies stringing jewelry. Surely these brightly colored necklaces would sell well here in Guatemala. We had these little bird fetishes from Taiwan, and we must have strung up ten or twelve thousand of those necklaces and sold them all over Guatemala. I supervised this while Dusty hired people to sell water purifiers. There was a definite need for this product and sales were going well until one day we received a registered letter, very official looking with stamps all over it, from someone in El Salvador.

"Before I explain the significance of the letter, let me say that in Central America most businesses run as monopolies. One family controls all the beer, one family controls all the cement for construction and so on. It's OK to be in business, just don't cut in on someone who's already staked their claim. People were known to disappear or be found with their throats slit.

"The man from El Salvador claimed in a very formal declaration that he had rights to all the Argenion water purifier sales in Central America, and that we had the choice of either turning over all our inventory and sales to him, or pay a hefty commission to him for every unit.

"Did Dusty get upset? No way. He called the President of Argenion in the United States and found that the guy in El Salvador wasn't any bigger than us. So, Dusty told his secretary to write a fuck you letter back to the man in El Salvador (in diplomatic Spanish of course) and we went on about our business.

• • •

BUSINESS WASN'T our only headache. As Bonnie can tell you, keeping a house in Guatemala was also a challenge.

"Since women were not well accepted in business in Latin American countries, I stayed at home more than I liked. Getting used to having maids was a real strain. And maids were necessary. It's not like home in the States. You can't do your own vacuuming because there's no wall to wall carpet. You can't do your own laundry because there aren't any washing machines. You can't shop for a week's groceries because of poor refrigeration—everything spoils in two to three days. So I learned that things must be done daily by maids with manual labor, over and over and over.

"At first, dealing with the maids was an exasperating experience for me. Spanish was a second language for them as well as me. The Indians speak their own Mayan dialects. Our first real language dilemma came about when I asked them what supplies they needed for cleaning the house. Escoba—broom, trapos—rags. Hey, we're doing great! Then came the word 'a-hocks.' This was not in the dictionary. We went through a game of charades trying to determine what 'a-hocks' was used for. The word turned out to be AJAX!! Everything in Guatemala is cleaned and scrubbed with Ajax. They use it for so many things you almost had to remind them no, it's NOT for washing my clothes, PREFERABLY not for dishes and by ALL means, not for washing the dog!

"Another little problem with Spanish, the day a truck driver came banging on the gate demanding 'flete.' That means freight. OK, no problem, something was arriving freight collect. But the guy showed me a bill for one hundred Quetzales, and demanded payment before he'd unload the cargo. When I questioned how big it was he said, 'Mmm, possibly five hundred kilos.' What in the world could we have ordered that weighed over one thousand pounds?

"By this time Dusty arrived and the driver vented his frustration in shouting, 'Mira senor, yo no puedo bajar su vaca sin paga.' Dusty laughed, said a few words in Spanish and the truck drove away. What was the cargo? A COW! The driver had the wrong address! Good thing, the landlord didn't even much like our dog. He sure would have hated a cow in our yard."

• • •

WE TRIED EVERYTHING we could think of to make money in Guatemala. We tried selling hooked rugs from the village of San Antonio, and pottery from San Cristóbal Totonicapán. The production of hook rugs fell off when a bridge collapsed and the weavers couldn't get materials. Pottery didn't do well because there was a flood up north. The water purifier business was slow because people had so little money to spend. We had sold all the silver fetish necklaces, and looked around for something else to sell.

I noticed that there were a lot of hummingbirds around our house, and I remembered the hummingbird feeders from Fun Valley and the red food the hummingbirds liked to drink. "Man," I thought, "those hummingbird feeders will sell here in Guatemala!"

I had Meyer Goldburg, a friend of mine in Denver, send me a few cases of the hummingbird feeders. We set some up on our porch and filled them full of that red liquid and waited. And waited. And waited. Those hummingbirds down there wouldn't go near the feeders. To this day, I don't know why.

Finally we decided to leave Guatemala. Why? It was pure economics. Our monthly expenses were more than our business income. The bright star that kept our spirits up was the fact that Mexico had just elected a new President. We knew we could start over in the saddleblanket business.

So long Guatemala, so long Negocios Guatejas. That was the name of our Guatemalan corporation. It was meant to translate Guatemala-Texas Trading Company. What we didn't realize was that in Guatemala *tejas* meant the heavy red roof tiles on their homes. To us *tejas* meant Texas and home. It was good to get back, and we became El Paso Saddleblanket soon after our return from Guatemala.

Chapter Ten

On the Road Again

*"We'd sell at the hotels and trading posts by day,
and hustle the trailer parks at night."*

 AFTER WE GOT BACK from Guatemala, we rented an apartment on the west side of El Paso. We started up production again in Juárez and put out our first catalog mailing. It was three color sheets, a lot smaller than the fifty-six-page catalog we put out these days. But I was thrilled to get back into using the mail to make sales.

Bonnie enjoyed getting back to civilization, and Sid loved that year. The backyard of our apartment building was two hundred acres of desert and every day he got to chase jack rabbits. We sold the Ford Econoline and bought a new Chevy Suburban and hit the road hard selling our products. When we were working a show at the famous Gene Autry Hotel on Palm Canyon Road in Palm Springs, California, we met an old cowboy named Bob Pruitt. Pruitt had been a champion professional rodeo cowboy in his younger years. After that he worked as a fearless Hollywood stunt man and performed at the Sahara Hotel in Las Vegas for many years. His stage show included trick roping, a bullwhip act, knife throwing and for a grand finale, wrestling a bear. Later, Pruitt put together a wild animal show and petting zoo. He was one crazy old man. He retired from performing and made a name for himself creating life-size fiberglass horses for Western wear shops, super-deluxe mobile dressing rooms for movie stars, and fancy, high-dollar horse trailers.

We needed a larger trailer to haul our merchandise, so we cut a deal with Pruitt and traded him wool doubleweave saddleblankets for this beautiful, custom-made, snazzy, glittery four-horse trailer that matched the color of our Suburban perfectly. Through the years, we got to be big friends with Pruitt. His ranch near San Bernadino, California became one of our regular stops and our part-time hangout. Among the many things I remember about Pruitt was that anytime we went to a restaurant, he would always order number one on the menu. Didn't matter what it was, just as long as it was first on the menu. And I learned never, ever to dare Pruitt to do ANYTHING. That crazy old son-of-a-bitch just didn't give a damn what he did, or said to anybody, anywhere, anytime.

WITH OUR NEW SUBURBAN and trailer, we hit the road. In those gypsy days, we continuously traveled a selling circuit, mostly in the Southwest. In the summer, we worked Santa Fe, Albuquerque, Denver, Colorado Springs, Dallas, Flagstaff and Durango. In the winter, we headed to Phoenix, Scottsdale, Tucson, Lake Havasu, Los Angeles, Palm Springs and San Francisco. Some cities we hit year round.

We followed a similar routine in each city. We placed an ad in the local paper announcing, "Dealers Wanted! Come to the show at the _____ Hotel! 12 noon." Then we mailed five hundred to a thousand postcards to stores and businesses. We used the same postcard for years, a photo of Bonnie standing in a huge room full of rugs and saddleblankets.

We usually booked a hotel banquet room for a two or three day rug show. We hired a few bellboys to help unload our horse trailer and set up all the displays. We pushed the tables against the walls and put chairs on top of them. Then we hung the big rugs from the top of the chairs, and we hung the small rugs from the edge of the tables.

As we traveled around doing rug shows, we gained the confidence of our customers. Gradually they trusted us to ship them merchandise sight unseen. So at every hotel show we weren't just soliciting new customers, we were also conducting our day-to-day business, shipping out orders in every direction. All the time we were on the road we had a friend and part-time secretary in El Paso answering our phone and checking our mailbox. So business went on normally wherever we were. Bonnie and I loved the fact that we weren't tied down to a phone and a location.

According to Bonnie's recollection, a typical day in Santa Fe went something like this: *"Rise early, dress, and go have a good green chile Mexican breakfast at Tia Sophia's. Dusty makes phone calls to local merchants, telling them we have something new they have to see—something they can really make a good profit on. I go straight to the showroom, pack any current orders and catch up on my bookkeeping. If old Sid—our German shepherd—is there, I take him for a run in the park. Midday is the busiest time when the merchants arrive. It is a real challenge trying to keep them apart. Small town shopkeepers are always jealous of each other. Once someone chooses a stack of rugs and puts something in their pile, it always catches someone else's eye, and they want it too. Fortunately, we almost always have plenty of each design for everyone, even if Dusty has led them to believe that they have a 'one of a kind' item.*

"Dusty is the salesman. I am the organizer and cashier. He tells stories and keeps smiling long after I reach total boredom. Some days, he plays games with customers just for our own entertainment.

"Some of the Santa Fe merchants were newcomers from New York and New Jersey. Their ultra-liberal attitudes are strange to us country folk. When Dusty and I think we've sold all we can possibly sell them, we take their money and start ruffling their feathers.

"Dusty leans back in a chair and sits scratching his stomach like an old southern redneck. 'Get those rugs loaded up for those folks,' he orders. You can almost feel the hair bristle as I obligingly throw fifty pounds of rugs over my shoulders. Little did they know that this was my preferred daily work out. Those women's libbers never caught on to our act. Probably one of the strongest components of our relationship is that we are able to have fun all the time we're working.

"After 7 or 8 P.M., we lock up the showroom and go for dinner at the Palace or some other really nice restaurant. Heck, we probably have more cash in our pockets

*than most of the so-called 'cultured tourists.' We are having fun, living high on the
hog and enjoying our independence."*

SANTA FE DURING AUGUST was exciting as the town overflowed with
movie stars and heavy weights from all over the U.S. Normally Old Sid
stayed at Fun Valley with my parents, but one time Old Sid ended up
with us at the Santa Fe Hilton during the high season. It made for some
interesting confrontations, as Bonnie recalls.

*"When we arrived at the hotel, I approached the desk clerk timidly and asked
in a whisper if my 120 pound German shepherd could share our room. Expecting
to be turned down, I was astounded when he boomed, 'That's no problem, Ma'am.
We've got an orangutan in room 301.'*

"It was true! Remember Clint Eastwood's co-star in the film Every Which
Way But Loose? *They were filming near Santa Fe. The orangutan not only had
a suite, but every morning a chauffeur-driven limo waited by the front door for
Clint's hairy co-star. The Hilton was crawling with young women hoping to catch
a glimpse of Clint Eastwood, but only the production crew was ever seen.*

*"Another great thing about August in Santa Fe was that Native American
tribal leaders from reservations and Native American communities all over the U.S.
gathered for Indian Market week. This gave us a chance to deal with Seminoles,
Utes, Ojibwas, Cherokees, Sioux and the members of other tribes from all over
America. We sell more than ever to our Native American clients, now that many of
them own thriving resorts and casinos."*

LOOKING THROUGH our scrapbooks from those years is amazing. One
town after another. Week after week. Sometimes we stayed in hotels.
At other times, we stayed in our travel trailer. But even when we were
staying in RV parks, relaxing after a show, we never stopped selling. I'd
always make a show of brushing off the rugs outside the trailer. Pretty
soon, someone would come up and ask what I was doing.

"Oh, just brushing off some rugs."

"Where'd you get them?"

"Oh, from Mexico. I'm an importer out here calling on some stores, and this is one of my samples."

"Where can we buy these rugs?"

"I don't know. I don't sell retail. Only wholesale."

"But couldn't we buy a few?"

"No, no. These are my samples."

"Ple-*a-s-e*..."

"Well, maybe since I'm going back to El Paso tomorrow, I could part with one or two..."

We'd sell at the hotels and trading posts by day, and hustle the trailer parks at night. We were young, energetic, and always looking for a sale. And in those days, we sold strictly for cash. We sometimes had as much as $100,000 in the travel trailer, which I kept in tin foil in the freezer. We were just gypsy traders, working the American highway.

OF COURSE, some days went better than others, as Bonnie will tell you.

"One weekend in Albuquerque, we wanted to get off to a good start, so we chose to visit a trader we thought would be a guaranteed sale. On this particular morning we chose Manny Goodman's famous Covered Wagon Store in the heart of Old Town Albuquerque. Manny greeted us warmly and gave us an order, so I went back to the horse trailer and pulled out thirty or so blankets. As I made my way clumsily back through the store with all this merchandise over my shoulder I took a wrong turn. Instead of going into the import section of the store where Manny was waiting, I got too close to Mrs. Goodman's sacred 'authentic Navajo Rug Room.'

"The strike of a rattlesnake could not have alarmed me more that ol' Mrs. Goodman's verbal assault. Seething and sputtering, she waved her hands wildly. Trinkets flew from the shelves and smashed on the floor. I lost my balance and dropped the blankets in a heap. Dozens of tourists in the packed shop eagerly helped me pick up the rugs. Much to Mrs. Goodman's surprise, the shoppers didn't hand the merchandise to me, they took it to the cash register. Almost every piece sold before it ever officially went into inventory. As Dusty and I left the store, we overheard quite a commotion from the back room as Mr. and Mrs. Goodman

conducted one of their infamous screaming matches. God rest her soul. She's gone now, but she wasn't one of my favorites. Unfortunately, nearly every little town has one phony 'Mrs. Goodman' type who runs a snooty, snobby gallery and conde-scends to everyone who doesn't share her taste.

"After that incident, Dusty and I needed a little fresh air, so we headed toward the Northern Indian pueblos. The day looked like it was going from bad to worse as a pick-up load of Indian women kept crowding us from the left, almost running us off the road. We stopped, hoping that they would pass by. They stopped too and approached us. What they wanted was for us to turn onto the road to Santo Domingo Pueblo and follow them to a house. There we found out that they wanted to purchase every rug we had with us. With a wad of cash in our pocket, we headed back to El Paso. That was enough excitement for one weekend!"

SOMETIME IN THE EARLY 1980s, we stopped doing our self-promoted hotel shows and began participating in organized trade shows. This was a costly change in our operation, but it helped us get to more cities in less time and gave us exposure to thousands of prospective buyers. The costs of a trade show run into the thousands of dollars when you add up the rent, freight, lighting, labor, etc. A foreign show can easily cost over $20,000.

In addition to the regular circuit of Western and gift shows in Phoenix, Los Angeles, Las Vegas, Denver and Dallas, we ventured at times to inter-national trade shows such as SPOGA and Equitana in Germany, the Calgary Stampede in Canada, Heimtextil in Frankfurt and Hanover, Germany, the Milan Fair and even a gift show in Japan.

For eight or nine years straight Bonnie and I had booths at the Las Vegas Western Show twice a year, every September and January. In addi-tion, we went out there for a few days a couple more times during the winter to meet the folks. I have never been one to gamble anywhere, especially in Las Vegas where I know I'm going to lose money—some-thing I would not enjoy. Bonnie never gambled.

As part of doing business, traditionally we made it a point to visit the local library to photocopy telephone yellow page listings of Western stores, trading posts, gift shops and other likely customers that we added to our mailing lists. One time in Las Vegas we asked a cab driver to take us to the library. He asked us if that was a bar or restaurant. He had been driving a cab there for many years but told us that was his first fare to any library. He had to call his dispatcher for directions.

My parents did a lot more gambling in Las Vegas than we ever did. Whenever they got the urge to splurge, they made trips to Las Vegas. During the early 1970s, they got to know the famous Texas gambler, Austin Preston, better known as "Amarillo Slim." Amarillo Slim was a super nice guy, who loved horses, dogs, kids and most of all loved to sit around and tell wild stories of his gambling adventures all over the world. He and Daddy were good friends. In the mid-'70s and all through the '80s, Daddy and Mother would spend part of the winter in Las Vegas playing poker and hanging out with Slim and other colorful characters.

Both my parents were good poker players. Mother played the smaller poker games and was always, always a consistent winner. Daddy played in the larger games. Sometimes Dad got into marathon games for twenty-four or thirty-six hours nonstop. He was well known and very popular with all the other gamblers at the Golden Nugget and the old MGM (now Bally's).

His problem was he was much better than the average hometown players but wasn't quite as skilled as the real Las Vegas pros. So for the most part he won in the medium games and then he lost his winnings in the bigger games. He justified that as winning since he did not lose his own money (or very much, anyway), a view that my mother and I did not share. Actually, my mother was a better, more disciplined gambler than my father.

Daddy was like thousands of other people, a wannabe actor. He did community theater for years, and out in Las Vegas, he somehow got small parts in two movies. He played a small role as a gambler in a film with Ryan O'Neal called *Fever Pitch*. He got another small role in a futuristic science fiction type movie called *Cherry 2000*. Both movies were box office flops, thus ending Daddy's longtime ambition of being a movie star.

Chapter Eleven

The Arizona Showroom

*"I got into the hammock business one time.
I was in Arizona. What do you hang
a hammock on in Arizona?"*

 IN OUR NEW CHEVY SUBURBAN with customized horse trailer, we continued to work our way around the Southwest hard-selling our products. We decided to set up a showroom in the Phoenix area. We quickly set up *three* showrooms. One was a wholesale showroom for saddleblankets and Mexican rugs. Another was the Navajo Rug Gallery in Scottsdale where we sold high-end Navajo rugs handwoven by the Navajo. The third was a wholesale gold jewelry distributorship.

The Navajo Rug Gallery was on West Main Street in the fine art gallery district of Scottsdale. We didn't have the gallery but about six months, then we wound up selling it to Tom Wheeler, a fifth generation Indian trader who owned the world-famous Hogback Trading Post in Waterflow, New Mexico. While we had the Navajo Rug Gallery we met a lot of the famous Western artists and sculptors, all the gallery owners and some big spending fat cats from everywhere.

One day Mr. and Mrs. Red Skelton walked into the Navajo Rug Gallery. Red was also an artist and specialized in oil paintings and sketches of clowns and some of the characters he portrayed. He was having a show and a print signing at one of the galleries. He wasn't really into Navajo Rugs, but I told him about the third business we had in Scottsdale, which was a wholesale gold jewelry and watch showroom. Red was interested and we quickly whisked him off to our gold jewelry showroom up the street at Scottsdale Oaks Plaza. Even though he was pretty elderly at the time he entertained all of us while Mrs. Skelton bought a lot of gold jewelry. He made a little drawing of a clown for Bonnie and signed it "Dear heart." Bonnie still has this framed and hanging in her office today.

HOW DID WE GET into the gold jewelry business? In about 1981, the Mexican rug business went through some bumps. The peso was overvalued against the dollar. We had a hard time getting good yarn. Business was pretty flat, things were not selling very well. Even though at that time we were the biggest maker and importer of Mexican rugs and blankets, we experimented with some other things in Scottsdale.

We got into the gold business when a fellow named Joel Morrow walked into our store. He was a gold jewelry manufacturer, an importer, and a Rolex watch dealer from Houston. We talked Joel into buying lots of Navajo rugs and being the salesman he is, he talked us into the gold jewelry business.

I'VE MET THOUSANDS OF PEOPLE so far on my journey: movie stars, billionaires, rock stars, famous artists, hustlers, cons, business people, etc. But bar none, the most interesting and complex person I have ever known is my friend, Joel Morrow.

I could probably write another book twice the size of this book, just about him. I have been trading with, selling to and buying from Joel nonstop ever since I've known him.

Joel was and is a tough, street smart dude that became a millionaire at a young age. What can I say? Joel is such a big, mean "pawnshop" type guy that wherever he spits, grass won't even grow there for about the next ten years. He is super honest. When you get his nod, you can take it to the bank. Everything in his life is extreme and always on the edge. After being around him a day or two, I always need at least a week off to just rest and sort things out in my own head and to rebuild, restore and repair anything that might have got in front of or near Joel.

Joel started out with a pawnshop in the seedy part of Houston. He knew all the angles of that business—all the crazies, and gangster types. Over the next few years, Joel accumulated about ten more pawnshops and became one of the largest Texas dealers of high-dollar jewelry, diamonds, gold watches and guns. The scrap gold coming in from all the pawnshops was melted down in his casting operation and cast into jewelry.

In the early 1980s, I became Joel's guy in Phoenix and in El Paso. We sold gold jewelry by weight and lots of used Rolex watches and accessories. Joel is a collector and trader of almost everything. Guns, jewelry, Indian rugs, baskets, you name it. He bought a $300,000 motor home. He even collected World War II tanks at his ranch mansion outside of Houston.

He was the ultimate money maker and money spender. He was not afraid of the Devil himself. He could be rude, mean and kindhearted, all at the same time. He was calculating, smart and sometimes reckless. He was an African safari hunter and adventurer who bagged elephants and tigers. In fact, about the only thing that could make Joel pee in his pants was shooting elephants as they charged him. He traded me zebra skins and all sorts of African items over the years.

Although I enjoyed the excitement of being around Joel, I never particularly liked the gold business. It was a dangerous business. You always had to keep looking over your shoulder, and I was always packing. Sometimes I would forget and walk into a bank or somewhere with my loaded 38. I was always dropping the damn thing.

Bonnie hated the gold and jewelry business and we eventually got out. Joel sold the pawnshops for about twenty million dollars and then went on a suicidal spending binge. He bought another beautiful river ranch in

Bay City and then proceeded to buy all the adjoining land. He had been dealing in gold jewelry and pistols in Italy for many years, but a few years ago he went to Russia and started more businesses in guns and God knows what else. He's still a great friend, loves El Paso and comes out here a lot with his wife, Lydia Ann. When he leaves, I always call him on his cell phone an hour or so after he goes, just to be sure he gets out of town so I can finally relax a little. I love this wild man and someday I might write a book about Mr. Morrow.

WHILE JOEL AND I were still in the gold business in Scottsdale, we started doing business with Troy Murray. Troy was a twenty-five year veteran of the West Main Street art gallery district in Scottsdale and probably the biggest dealer of western art in the world. He was one of the best salesmen I've ever met, and he was super smooth with the rich folk. He was a real charmer, and we became big buddies almost from the time we met. Not only did we refer business to each other, but Troy and I sold a lot of gold jewelry and Rolex watches to his big customers. He was a stand up, honest guy, and we worked great together. He was already very wealthy but loved to sell and hustle.

I remember Troy had this cocky young guy who had just inherited a huge fortune. Troy stroked him and had the guy eating out of his hand. He loved Troy and Troy "helped" this guy find great art. This guy also loved gold. He often flew in from Las Vegas in his private jet with all his high rolling friends, and it was "Christmas" for us whenever he came around.

One day, the normally happy-go-lucky Troy came into our Navajo Rug Gallery with a long, sad face. Our big-spending buddy and some of his high rollin' friends had just crashed their jet in the side of the Grand Canyon. Christmas had just come to an end for Troy and Dusty. Troy is retired now and we still keep in touch. He was the best at what he did.

• • •

WHILE WE WERE BASED in Phoenix, we looked around to try to expand our rug production and decided to try and set up a production facility in the U.S. I sold a few rugs to a guy who had a lot of experience setting up training programs on American Indian reservations. We talked and decided to try and set up a rug weaving facility for the Pasqua Yaqui tribe outside of Tucson.

At that time, the Pasqua Yaqui were a desperately poor people from Mexico that had just been recognized as a Native American tribe here in the U.S. They were so poor that the only way they could earn money was by selling bags of charcoal.

Our idea was to get funding to train the Pasqua Yaqui to weave and set up a manufacturing facility on their reservation. But as we pursued the project, we began to feel uncomfortable. The guy we were working with was everything we always kind of despised about the ultra-liberals. He was really nothing more than a professional grant writer who figured that the government owed him and everyone else a living.

His idea was to get as much training money as possible, even though the program he proposed was completely unrealistic. When we said that the Pasqua Yaqui we trained under his plan wouldn't be able to support themselves by weaving just for us, the guy blew us off and said, "That's OK. We'll worry about that later." This guy knew where to get money from the Catholic Church, from CETA, from a whole bunch of government sources, but he didn't have any idea how to set up a business. Once the training money was gone, he would be on to the next grant, and we would be left with a bunch of underemployed weavers.

Even though we felt uncomfortable about the deal, we went along with it. Our political beliefs have never gotten too much in the way of making money, which is true for most people. We were going to put in a weaving factory and set up mobile homes and help the Pasqua Yaqui go from zero to something.

We almost went ahead with the deal. But just at that time, the Seminole Indians hit it big with high stakes bingo. They made so much money that they were able to approach other tribes to set up bingo operations. They financed bingo among the Pimas and the White River Apaches.

Then they financed a bingo operation among the Pasqua Yaquis. Instead
of weaving, the Pasqua Yaquis did bingo—and made millions of dollars.
In the end, the Indian bingo and gambling operations actually helped
El Paso Saddleblanket. Today, Indian casinos are some of our biggest
customers.

BONNIE RECALLS, *"By 1982, we were getting a little road weary. Along with
running the Scottsdale business, we had managed to put another 100,000 miles
on the Suburban, going to shows and seeing customers. We did not want to become
like some of the older salesmen we knew. A salesman on the road is like the tread
on your tires. You only have so much tread, and eventually you wear it down.*

*"We felt our own tread wearing down and decided to change our operations.
We opened a wholesale showroom in Phoenix at 2424 East Indian School Road.
Although we owned a comfortable house in Scottsdale, we found it much more
practical to skip the traffic and move into the basement apartment below the
warehouse. We continued to commute back and forth to El Paso, but living beneath
the warehouse proved to be the most productive period of our entire career. We
worked eighteen hours a day and had more energy than ever. After supper, we went
back up to the office and worked until midnight. Dusty did the advertising and
promotional work, I did the books, and Sid and his new girlfriend Sadie chased
around the showroom playing tag and rolling wildly in the Peruvian Alpaca rugs.*

*"We managed to significantly increase our customer base by mass mailings and
the addition of toll free 800 telephone lines. Dennis Rice came on board with us
in 1983 and helped us perfect the art of follow-up phone calls to customers. Today,
he is still with us.*

*"One of the worst things about operating from Arizona was that the East
Coast customers called at 6 A.M.! We could barely communicate with them anyway, between Dusty's West Texas drawl and their East Coast accent.*

*"Finally in 1984, all signs were 'go' to set up back home in El Paso. We found
a place for ourselves and our inventory at 5000 Alameda Street, on old Highway
80, and we opened a large wholesale showroom. Finally, El Paso Saddleblanket
Company had a Texas address, and we settled in to make the most of it."*

Chapter Twelve

Alameda Street Store

"You don't make your money buying. You make your money selling.
If you're a good enough salesman,
it doesn't matter what kind of a buyer you are."

 OUR NEW WAREHOUSE on Alameda Street was actually in the first strip shopping center ever built in El Paso, right across the street from the old Del Camino Motel. It wasn't a luxury location. Our landlord was an older Greek/Mexican gentleman named Miguel Papadopolous. His family was from Torreon, Mexico. He was a tough old character. One time, when I was negotiating to rent some additional space, we stood inside the warehouse property and talked about air conditioning.

"I'll need to have air conditioning in this space," I told him.

"I will get you air conditioning," Papadopolous said.

"Well," I suggested, "Maybe it would be good if we wrote it down in a contract."

"Write it down!" Papadopolous yelled. "Write it down! I will write it down!" He picked up a pencil and started writing on the wall of the warehouse. "Air conditioning." Then he turned to me. "What else do you want me to write down?"

We didn't wash off that wall until he delivered on his promise.

• • •

LIKE I SAID, the Alameda Street location wasn't the best neighborhood in town. There was a methadone clinic two doors down, a halfway house for convicts just out of jail across the street, and a pretty big number of transients and junkies who hung around the place. When we first moved into the location, I noticed a group of guys hanging around the front door. I decided it was time to make a point. So I took out my 22 pistol, stepped out of the store, looked up at the telephone line and started blasting away at the pigeons. I think I made my point because we never had any trouble with anybody in all our years at Alameda Street.

In fact, I used to hire them to help unload trucks and clean up around the warehouse. The last thing the halfway house guys wanted was to get in trouble again and the first thing the junkies wanted was a couple of bucks for their next fix. Some were bums, but a lot were decent people who just got a little out of step with society.

AT ALAMEDA STREET, I learned a lot about selling. If you have ever seen a good jewelry salesman, you know there is a certain way they hold the jewelry, a certain way they present it that makes it attractive to the buyer. Taking buyers through the warehouse, I sharpened my skills at presenting the saddleblankets, rugs, and other merchandise. I developed a way of talking, a way of moving my hands, a way of handling the merchandise.

The art here is to come across very politely and never be arrogant in any way. It's the old, "I really wish I could, I really, really do, because you seem like a great salesman and buyer and I think we could work together well…"

Usually, I like to walk a potential buyer through our shipping department to show how much and where we are shipping. I like to say, "Man, I wish you were my buyer. I can see why you are so successful. Your company is really lucky to have you…"

There have only been a few times when I've handled a buyer one-on-one and he has walked away without buying. Through the years, I have developed a reputation for being fair, very independent and most of all, POLITE. On Alameda Street I learned that a key to making a sale is to make the person you are dealing with feel important. You will never gain anything by putting people down.

I used to deal with a lot of Mexican vendors coming up to the Alameda Street warehouse and selling off their trucks. Making the deal usually followed the same script.

First, I always took a long, slow look at the merchandise. While I looked, I talked politely with the vendor. Most important, I never asked about price before I gave the "sermon." At the end of the sermon, I told the vendor, "I don't like to play games. In fact, I won't play games with you because I think you may be a lot smarter than I am. We both more or less know what the prices are on your merchandise. So here's what we'll do. Take your time and quote me the best price and I'll tell you yes or no."

If the vendor actually heard and believed what I said, he quoted me a real good price, and I said, "*Hecho*" (done/made). But most of the time, he gave me a bad price and I said, "No, thank you," and abruptly walk off.

Next, the shocked vendor chased after me saying maybe a better price or something about why his first price was so high. I acted a little offended but not mad and told him that by not first offering me his best price, he had disappointed me by not being honest. Then I started to soften up a little by saying that since he didn't know me, I could maybe understand why he wasn't up-front with me. "Look," I told him. "I tell you what. Go across the street to the Del Camino Motel. Get a room and tell them to charge it to me. Rest a little. I think you had a long hard drive from the interior." Then jokingly I always said, "You need to let your eyes rest because when you were in line coming over the bridge from Mexico, the reflection of the gold you saw must have hurt your eyes."

Then I always joked around with him in a very respectful way, adding a little of the jive-boys talk and Spanish slang. I talked silly, refused to discuss the deal and acted like I was trying to say good-bye.

Right before I left, I looked him in the eye for a long time and said dead serious, "OK. If you want to get serious and give me the best price

I will be back in thirty minutes because I have to make a very important phone call."

Probably about seventy-five percent of the time I made a deal right then. If I didn't, I thanked the vendor and told him that we almost had a deal and the prices were good overall but the price on this, this and this should be X amount. Why doesn't he go along with this and then I'll cut him a check? If not, I told him that next time maybe I could pay the price he asked, but not today. At this point, I got my way ninety-five percent of the time.

I also learned a lot about employees. We never had many until we set up shop at Alameda Street. It was difficult at first to figure out how to train our employees, but eventually we figured it out. Some of the employees who started with us on Alameda Street are still with us today. I guess we're doing something right.

Now, I've done a bunch of dumb things in my life but I have done a few smart things too. And, I must admit, one of the best things I've done was to figure out how to fix a problem I was having with my weavers in Juárez.

I have been dealing with weavers for a lifetime. Weavers are strange people. They have a kind of blue-collar mentality combined with the emotions and sensitivity of an artist. And to add to that, most of the weavers that I work with in Juárez are "cholo" types: long haired, tattooed, street smart, tough guys. You go into their workshop and there's heavy metal music playing.

Anyway, for years we had a problem with yarn. The weavers were all stealing yarn. They made sweaters with it or sold it or whatever. For years and years I told them, "Look, you can steal some yarn but don't be stealing over your quota or we're gonna have to fire you or do something about it."

My threats didn't do much good, and I wrassled with the problem for years. Then one day I came up with a plan. I decided to sell the weavers yarn at a high price and buy it back from the weavers at the same price according to weight (the weight of the merchandise plus the scraps). I figured that if I did that, then the weavers could steal all the yarn they wanted, and I would make money on what they were stealing.

My plan worked like a charm. The weavers stopped stealing yarn. The only thing I had to watch for was that the weavers didn't dump extra yarn into their pile of scraps to boost the weight. It solved my problem completely.

WE STARTED WITH the corner store at Alameda Street, then expanded and expanded until we took up almost the entire old shopping center. We began mailing thousands of wholesale catalogs and using a new concept for business called the toll free watts line. Our Alameda Street warehouses were bulging with tack and saddles from Mexico, rugs and blankets, rustic furniture, curios, Oriental rugs, hides and skins from all over the world, Indian pottery, and baskets. In those days we were also importing container loads of Belgium rugs and Philippine products. Traders were driving in from New York, Alaska, Florida and everywhere else to load up and take back merchandise by the truckloads! It was an exciting growth period.

Chapter Thirteen

World Famous Trading Post

*"I think of that freeway out there as a big ol' river full of fish.
I'm sitting here with a cane pole dangling my hook in it,
and every once in a while I'll pull one of 'em in."*

IN 1987 we moved El Paso Saddleblanket from Alameda Street to downtown. At our new 36,000-square-foot location on Oregon Street another fascinating change took place. For the first time THE PUBLIC WALKED IN! Although we really liked the wholesale part better, we readily adapted to the retail business. We quickly became one of El Paso's major tourist attractions. The downtown location became famous for offering reservation Indian jewelry, fine Oriental rugs and decorative items from every corner of the world.

The retail world was exciting but a lot of work. We had to increase our staff, keep longer hours, and take on a much more public profile than we had before. Our way of doing business had to change too. We weren't just traders anymore. We were operators of a world famous trading post.

• • •

ONE OF THE THINGS WE NEEDED for the retail business was advertising. I looked around at various options. For some reason, billboards caught my fancy. We had a huge flow of traffic moving through El Paso and, as it turned out, some of my old customers who owned trading posts were also in the billboard business so I could deal with them.

Billboards are like anything else. You've got to get a good price on them or they won't work for you. I just would never go out and pay the first asking price on them. I got a deal with the Bowlin Company. They were old trading post owners and had hundreds of billboards. Eventually the billboards got to be a bigger business than the trading post. I'd known Mr. Bowlin for fifteen years, and I worked a deal with him. I got a super low price on the condition that if he got a real player I got booted off the billboard. It's kind of like selling empty seats on an airplane. He had the right to throw me out at any time and vice versa. I also traded him tons of merchandise for the billboard space.

WHEN WE STARTED the billboard deal, I had to learn about how they worked. At first, I wrote down a whole laundry list of items I wanted on the billboards. The billboard salesman called me up and said, "Well, Mr. Henson, maybe you want to put less words up on your billboard. You know it's hard to read things when you're traveling at seventy miles an hour."

I said, "Look, you're just getting lazy. Now I'm paying for it, and you do what I'm paying you to do. Don't tell me what to do…"

He went ahead and painted the billboard just like I wanted it. I drove by and shook my head. Sure enough, I couldn't read anything. I called the guy back and said, "You're right…"

Some of the phrases that worked best on our billboards were "World Famous Trading Post," "Worldwide Import/Export," and "50,000 Rugs in Stock."

Eventually, I was paying over $10,000 a month for billboards. We had them up north of Santa Fe, between Tucson and Phoenix, outside

Alamogordo and as far east as Sweetwater, Texas. "It pays to advertise," I told the reporter in an interview for the *El Paso Times*. "El Paso is a great place. We have a lot of neat things here, and people need to know it. It's not exactly all out of the goodness of my heart that I do this. I have a profit motive too. I see this freeway as a river, with a lot of fish in it. They say some sixty million people drive through each year. The trick is to pull out a fishing pole and bring 'em in."

In one year, we spent $500,000 advertising El Paso Saddleblanket Company, forty-seven percent more than the city's own $340,000 promotional budget. "Dusty Henson spends more money advertising El Paso than we do," said Tom Caradonio, executive director of the El Paso Convention, Civic Center and Tourism Department.

Of course, some folks here in El Paso kidded me because of the billboards. But they worked to pull in customers. People often asked me, "Dusty, how many billboards you got?" Because I had so many of them and so many different deals, I always had to say, "Well, I honestly don't know."

I LEARNED that you had to watch some of the billboard guys. They can be pretty ruthless and cutthroat. Some of them will go out and sell one board to two or three different people. They can get away with it because people don't go out to check on the billboards.

One day I was sitting in the office when the phone rang. It was an old rancher on the line, and he was pissed off. "I'm comin' down there," he snarled. "And I'm gonna kick your ass."

"What about?"

"You put up a sign on my property without permission and I told that other guy before that I..."

"Now, wait a minute, wait a minute," I interrupted. "Let's talk about this other guy..."

The old rancher explained the situation and I said, "Now you've gotta understand, sir. This is not my sign. I didn't paint it. I haven't even seen it. I think some ass needs to be kicked, but why don't you go to this guy who owns the billboard and deal with him? Then you come down here, and I'll sell you a saddleblanket at wholesale price and we'll get along just fine. Now I totally sympathize with your position, but I didn't do it…" The rancher never did come down to buy a saddleblanket, but he never called me again, either.

WE GOT INTO a whole bunch of other promotions to help the retail business. One of the things we launched was the El Paso Saddleblanket Chili Cook-Off and Bean Cook-Off in Downtown El Paso. We donated the proceeds to the Americana Museum at the El Paso Civic Center Plaza.

We helped sponsor the International Paris to Panama Motorcycle Rally stop in El Paso. The city turned down a request to spend $2,648 on entertainment and T-shirts to promote El Paso in conjunction with the event. I liked the idea of the event so I covered the expense. My good friend Sherman Barnett owns the El Paso Harley Davidson, which is the largest Harley distributor in the world, believe it or not (this is not a misprint, the world's largest Harley dealership is in El Paso, Texas). He was into the event, so I pitched in the money necessary to sponsor it. "These kind of events help get our name out there," I explained to the press at the time. "We're giving away one thousand arrowheads at the rodeo in conjunction with another promotion, and it's the same sort of thing."

We tried some interesting in-store promotions as well. For the first several years of our retail operation, we had a live weaving demonstration everyday. We had a big loom set up in the store, and a full-time weaver working. One year, we even took the weaver to the International Western Show in Denver and had a weaving demonstration in one of our booths.

We made sure El Paso Saddleblanket got plenty of airtime on TV and radio. I got a good deal on late night cable TV ads here in El Paso. Sometimes late at night our commercials would be on thirty channels at once. And we got great radio advertisement rates thanks to our friends at the Jim Phillips Radio Empire as well.

• • •

ALONG WITH THE BILLBOARDS and all the other promotions, we expanded our three-page catalog. I got a big kick out of the catalog, and I still do. To me, sending out the catalog is a lot like playing a slot machine in Vegas. Only backwards. The more money you put in, the more money comes out. You'll get it back. Now you may starve to death waiting for it to come back, but it will come back to you eventually.

What started as a small, simple catalog grew over the years. We started to include more images, and more pages. Over the years our catalog has proven to be our most reliable source of advertising. These days, every quarter we mail out about 250,000 copies of our new, fifty-six-page, full-color wholesale catalog to stores all across the country and the world.

I'm a believer in advertising. I particularly like what I call "non-vanishing" advertising. To me, radio and TV—it just kinda goes out into space or something. At least somebody could find an old copy of my catalog in some cave, or old mine shack, you know, five hundred years from now. Print advertising just doesn't go away. And what goes around comes around eventually.

There's a famous story about Mr. Wrigley, the chewing gum magnate. He was traveling on a train with a newly hired Harvard business whiz kid. The kid said to Mr. Wrigley that since business was going so well, they should cut back on advertising or cut it out for a long time. Mr. Wrigley pointed out that the train was going along at about seventy miles an hour, and if they cut the engine from the cars, the train would continue to go seventy miles an hour...FOR A WHILE. Also it is said that fifty percent of all advertising is wasted, BUT WHICH FIFTY PERCENT?

Chapter Fourteen

Making Deals

"Listen to your business. It'll talk to you."

WE'VE BEEN TRADING MERCHANDISE every day for over forty years. But we have always kept our eyes, ears and noses open for new products. Merchandise is like the weather in Texas—it changes constantly. What sells today won't necessarily sell tomorrow, and that means you should jump at the chance to make money today.

When we consider adding a new product, we have to consider a few basic questions. Will the product sell? Will the product sell at the right price? And is there a good supply of the product?

One of our best-selling items over the years has been pottery. I've always liked pottery. It's got a handmade feeling to it, just like handwoven fabric. And it's tied into the history of the Southwest. So I have always been on the lookout for well-made pottery.

One day in 1984, a fellow walked into our Alameda location from the interior of Mexico. Oscar Quezada was his name, and he was carrying a wicker grain basket. He came into our store, unpacked his basket and showed us a new style of pottery that we had never seen before, even with all our travels in Mexico. I liked the new pottery immediately. Oscar called it Casas Grandes.

Actually, Casas Grandes pottery was first introduced about one thousand years ago in an area of Northern Mexico called Paquime. Although at first the pots were crude utilitarian vessels, their style, shape and quality improved through trade with the Hohokam and Anasazi people. Paquime pottery featured stylized bird and leaf patterns and was somewhat similar to the pottery of the Northern Pueblos, but was distinct in that it featured very thin walls. The Paquime culture peaked sometime in the thirteenth or fourteenth century and then vanished.

A young man who grew up near the Paquime ruins took great interest in the pottery shards of his ancestors. Now world renowned, Juan Quezada worked tirelessly for many years, not just to bring back what was, but to take the art of pottery to new heights.

Juan Quezada shared his techniques with family and friends until the revival of pottery making became an industry for his village. This industry required a market. After Oscar Quezada first walked into our store, members of the Quezada family brought truckload after truckload of their work to El Paso Saddleblanket Company, and we are proud to say that we helped them develop their market.

While museums and snob galleries clamored for the pieces signed by Juan himself, El Paso Saddleblanket provided an outlet for the tens of thousands of pots produced by aspiring artists. Juan Quezada and his sisters still drop by El Paso Saddleblanket at least once a year to visit with Bonnie and me.

Here we are in the twenty-first century selling articles that are a revival of a fourteenth century craft, and there is a tremendous market. Just like handweaving, handcrafted pottery is another art that people cherish and want to preserve. It is also an art that has been influenced through history by trade and traders. It's an art that responds to the marketplace. And our job as traders is to help that art survive. Today we still offer two grades of pottery from the Casas Grandes region: Casas Grandes and the higher grade Paquime.

• • •

SOMETIMES, I've come up with simple marketing ideas that have made products fly off the shelves. Take freeze-dried piranhas for instance. I came across a dealer of freeze-dried piranhas while I was traveling the Amazon in Brazil. They were kind of gruesome looking things with big jaws and nasty teeth. Well, I bought some, but they weren't selling real well until I had two cards made up and hung them from their mouths. One of the cards said, "Hello, I'm your lawyer and I'm here to help you." And the other card said, "Hello, I'm from the IRS and I'm here to help you."

Just that little marketing gimmick made all the difference, and I couldn't buy enough freeze-dried piranhas to satisfy the demand. Then, I couldn't get any piranhas at all. Brazil started protecting the Amazon crocs, and the Amazon crocs ate the piranhas, so the Brazilians started protecting piranhas and made it illegal to sell them freeze-dried. Oh well.

THE MOST IMPORTANT THING TO DO when introducing a new product is to start off with fair prices at both ends. I really like to pay as much as possible to the vendor and sell as low as possible to the customer. There is usually still plenty of room to make money. I always start at what I can sell something for and work backwards letting everyone make as much as possible. And I seldom look at, or care about, what the competition is doing.

I have all kinds of ways of getting ahold of merchandise. We have people who bring it to me—these people are called pickers. We also have full-time help in Mexico City, Chihuahua and Oaxaca. And I also have business relationships where people send me stuff every week or two weeks or so.

Although I have many different arrangements with suppliers and traders, I am always amazed at the similarities between the social systems in craft villages around the world. Whether I am setting up a trade arrangement with a village of weavers in Guatemala or a village of potters in Mexico, I always begin by finding "Mr. Wonderful." Who is Mr. Wonderful? He is the villager who is a little more successful and a little more ambitious than his neighbors. He is the villager whose home is a little nicer, and whose workshop is a little neater than all the others in the village. Mr. Wonderful is the villager who runs a store in the front of his home or who has collected some surplus inventory which he is eager to sell. Almost every craft village in the world has a Mr. Wonderful, and he is the person with whom I set up my trading relationship.

Just as there is a Mr. Wonderful in every village, so there will inevitably be a crisis in dealing with every Mr. Wonderful. The crisis usually comes six months to a year after the product pipeline has started to flow, when Mr. Wonderful begins to demand higher prices or threatens to sell all of his inventory to another trader. Whenever I set up a relationship with a Mr. Wonderful, I warn him in advance that this crisis is going to come. I let Mr. Wonderful know that I will always treat him fairly and that it is in his best interest to treat me fairly as well. That kind of understanding has allowed me to build successful relationships with Mr. Wonderfuls in villages around the world.

WE NEVER TRIED to sell anyone's culture or traditions because, frankly, most people don't give a damn. Most of our customers are American consumers. We are part of the "me" generation. We are only interested in one thing—what can this product do for ME? How will it look in MY house? How much money can I save? Will MY friends think I am cool?

We have always had good luck with finding an arts and crafts form (such as weaving, pottery, woodcarving, saddles, etc.) made somewhere and redesigning it for the U.S. market. We change it to improve the quality and to make it more attractive to the American market. Once we have done this, we have a product that no one else has, and we can usually offer a lower price than the original style we started with.

MANY AMERICANS stereotype Mexicans and make a lot of generalizations about Mexico. What Americans fail to understand is that Mexico is very similar to the U.S. It is a country made up of different regions with different cultures, different foods and different languages. Just as in the United States, the people from different areas of Mexico sometimes conflict with one another. For instance, some folks in Juárez have joke bumper stickers on their cars that say in Spanish, "Kill some one from Mexico City. It's patriotic."

I like to say that Mexico City is the New York City of Mexico. Both cities are huge, powerful, exciting, beautiful, ugly, wonderful and dangerous. Many Mexicans, for whatever reasons, don't like Mexico City or its inhabitants, just as many Americans don't like New York City or New Yorkers. The slang name *chilango* refers to people from Mexico City much in the same unflattering way that southerners refer to New Yorkers as Yankees. I personally love New York and Mexico City, and I love doing business in both cities.

You can go to any major bookstore and find all the usual books on arts and crafts of Mexico. These books are usually written by some know-it-all, self-proclaimed expert on Mexico, maybe a Spanish teacher who traveled around for a couple of weeks during the summer. Many wannabe importers purchase these books, travel around buying small quantities of various arts and crafts from remote places, then write cute little descriptions of each craft followed by "more-than-you-want-to-hear" background information. These wannabe importers end their descriptions with gushing glorifications of themselves as heroes who have saved a craft tradition from becoming extinct. Most of these people have unrealistic or nonexistent marketing plans, spend all their money on travel expenses and are almost always out of business after the maiden voyage.

I guess I could say "been there, done that." After putting the *lápiz* (pencil) to it, I quickly figured out that a gathering system of traveling to rural areas and buying handicrafts could not come close to working. Also, the areas with the most concentrated arts and crafts production in Mexico, such as Guadalajara, Oaxaca and San Miguel de Allende, are also major tourist areas where the importer must compete for products with waddling tourists in shorts with cameras around their necks. Because of this, most of the artisans in those areas develop a retail/tourist mindset and are difficult or impossible to deal with.

Nowadays, we manufacture or contract most of our own products, but in the early days we were the largest and about the only major volume importer of native Mexican arts and crafts at the time?

Why were we more successful than most of the other people running around all over Mexico trying to do business? The answer was MEXICO CITY, the capitol city of over twenty-four million people. Mexico City is a cosmopolitan and industrial city that was certainly not famous for small-village-type arts and crafts.

We were familiar with Mexico City as a layover place for airplane flights but not as a source for arts and crafts. That was before we met Rudolfo Martinez. Rudolfo was a Mexico City computer programmer whose late father had been a smalltime peddler of baskets, pottery, onyx, leather goods and other crafts around Mexico. Bonnie and I partnered with young Rudolfo and opened a warehouse in his old barrio neighborhood in the central part of Mexico City. Rudolfo moved both his small computer business and his mother into a small warehouse on 5th of February Street. Rudolfo had the ambition and the contacts, and Mama watched over her "two sons, Rudolfo and Dusty." Doing business with the protection of a Mexican *mamacita* is hard to describe, but if you are Hispanic, you will know what I'm talking about. She was great, rest her soul. I still think about her often.

What we discovered was that many, many poor people of Mexican-Indian origin had immigrated to Mexico City in search of factory jobs. Being from various craft producing villages all over the Republic, many moonlighted with the craft skills they had learned back in their native villages. And whenever they became unemployed, they worked at their crafts full-time. In fact, the outlying areas of Mexico City were almost like villages in themselves, with populations from remote locations that still practiced their traditional arts and crafts.

We set up and promoted all kinds of back-street workshops making every type of product you could imagine. The subway was only a peso or two from anywhere in the city to our central area warehouse. Usually Friday was the day we received the week's production. After we had accumulated a large truck full, we would blast off for El Paso. Thanks to

Rudolfo, everything was accurate and computerized, and the pipeline from the interior to the border was in full flow for fifteen years or so. As we gradually got into more and more of our own manufacturing and our Rancho El Cid project, we closed down our operation in Mexico City. Rudolfo is now a big shot computer executive, and our old 5th of February Street warehouse is now a funeral parlor.

SOME OF THE THINGS I've traded for haven't wound up in our catalog or our showroom. For a while, I was big into trading for antique Cadillacs. I had one of every Cadillac from 1949 to 1961 and two of a couple of them, sixteen altogether. I don't know why I traded for them. I just liked them. And I figured they'd be worth something sometime.

One Monday morning in 1988, a guy called me at the store. He was a real smooth guy, a real good talker. "Mr. Henson," he said. "I have seen your old cars and you seem like a gentleman of good taste. I myself believe I share your taste, and I have something that you might be interested in."

"Sure," I said. "Whaddya got? Rugs, old cars..."

"I've got a house."

I said, "Sir, I don't do real estate of any kind. I don't do stocks or savings bonds. I'm strictly a merchandise guy."

He said, "Let me tell you about this house, Mr. Henson. This may be something that you want for yourself."

"I got the house I'm gonna be in the rest of my life," I told him. It was a great California mission-style house on Silver Street in central El Paso. But this old boy got to telling me about the house he had. The elevator. The stained glass window. A four level, five bedroom house on five big lots built in 1916—7,200 square feet. He got my interest up. I told Bonnie, "Look, let's go over and meet this guy. He's gonna show us this house and if you like it, you give me a nod because I think I can deal with him..."

So we go over to the house. I remember I looked at my watch. It was about eleven in the morning. We looked around, and Bonnie gave me a nod. Twenty-nine minutes later, we had a deal.

It was a pretty complex deal. I wrote down the list of seven old Cadillacs I was going to trade the guy, and I threw in a couple U-hauls of merchandise and some wooden Indians. I agreed to assume the note and a small second he had. We also wound up buying a lot of the furniture, plus I gave him $20,000 green cash. That Friday, while they were moving out, we were moving in. Bonnie and I still live in the house we traded for, and we love it.

WITH ALL THE PRODUCTS we've sold, all the deals we've made, we've stuck to one rule: always listen to your business.

Being successful is easy if you listen to your business. So many people don't. They get a "gallery" mentality. They try to sell merchandise *they* like instead of merchandise *their customers* like. If people keep asking for black saddles and all you've got is brown, get some black ones. That's listening to your business.

PHOTO
Scrapbook

1947 – 2007

Ready to make a deal—age three, in 1947.

Bonnie Jean Vetterick at age two, 1950.

The Henson kids—myself (on left), Melba and Bennie—July 27, 1951.

Henson's Fun Valley Resort, South Fork, Colorado, 1966.

Private 1st Class Henson, Fort Hood, Texas, 1966. I was an ambulance driver in the U.S. Army.

ABOVE: Old West Hotel in Del Norte, Colorado, 1970. LEFT: Gambler "Amarillo Slim" (on left) and actor Alberto Bosco, Old West Hotel, 1970.

My dad, Mack Henson, while making a movie in Las Vegas, Nevada, 1985.

My mother and dad, Jean and Mack Henson, 1993.

LEFT: The brochure Mauricio introduced in 1975 showed Mexican rugs being made on upright looms. We changed our advertising to correctly show Mexican rugs being made on horizontal looms as pictured above.

BELOW: Our first postcard/invitation advertising hotel rug shows was black and white, 1976.

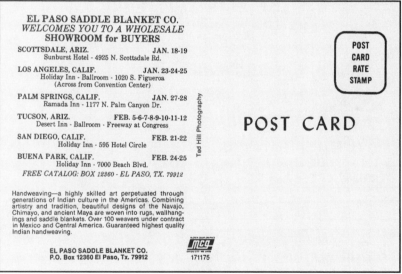

EL PASO SADDLE BLANKET CO.
WELCOMES YOU TO A WHOLESALE
SHOWROOM for BUYERS

SCOTTSDALE, ARIZ.   JAN. 18-19
    Sunburst Hotel - 4925 N. Scottsdale Rd.

LOS ANGELES, CALIF.   JAN. 23-24-25
    Holiday Inn - Ballroom - 1020 S. Figueroa
    (Across from Convention Center)

PALM SPRINGS, CALIF.   JAN. 27-28
    Ramada Inn - 1177 N. Palm Canyon Dr.

TUCSON, ARIZ.   FEB. 5-6-7-8-9-10-11-12
    Desert Inn - Ballroom - Freeway at Congress

SAN DIEGO, CALIF.   FEB. 21-22
    Holiday Inn - 595 Hotel Circle

BUENA PARK, CALIF.   FEB. 24-25
    Holiday Inn - 7000 Beach Blvd.

FREE CATALOG: BOX 12360 - EL PASO, TX. 79912

Handweaving—a highly skilled art perpetuated through
generations of Indian culture in the Americas. Combining
artistry and tradition, beautiful designs of the Navajo,
Chimayo, and ancient Maya are woven into rugs, wallhangings and saddle blankets. Over 100 weavers under contract
in Mexico and Central America. Guaranteed highest quality
Indian handweaving.

EL PASO SADDLE BLANKET CO.
P.O. Box 12360 El Paso, Tx. 79912   171175

Ted Hill Photography

POST
CARD
RATE
STAMP

POST CARD

*Our first color postcard. This is a typical front and back design of some of the
thousands of postcards we mailed out promoting hundreds of "on the road"
hotel shows we did from 1974 through 1981.*

Ad for a hotel show in Guatemala City, Guatemala, 1977.

Examples of classified ads we placed during the late '70s.

After 8 months of living and working with our weavers in Mexico and Central America, I'm happy to say this year's inventory is the largest and best ever. In addition to the wool rugs in the catalog, we have now developed a line of beautiful Chimayo design acrylic rugs and wallhangings, traditional Saltillo style serapes, and combed wool Quiche Indian blankets from Guatemala. These will be cataloged soon — please write for more information. Also, please notice on the enclosed catalog that our prices have not increased since January, 1976. If you happen to be in Arizona this winter, plan to come to one of our shows and see everything that's new. Let me hear from you,

Dusty

4th WINTER SEASON ARIZONA SHOWROOM FOR DEALERS

Oct. 26   Camelback Sahara Hotel — Phoenix, Az
Nov. 2-3   Sands Hotel — Tucson, Az.
Nov. 15-16   Sunburst Hotel — Scottsdale, Az.
Dec. 2-3-4   Sands Hotel — Tucson, Az.
Dec. 14-15   Camelback Sahara Hotel — Phoenix, Az.

Dusty Henson   •   *P.O. Box 12360*   •   *El Paso, Texas 79912*

WHOLESALE   •   JOBBER
SHOWROOM for DEALERS

Wednesday, October 26, 9 a.m. - 9 p.m.
Camelback Sahara Hotel — Dunes Roo
502 W. Camelback — **Phoenix,** Az.

NEW PRODUCTS — NEW DESIGI

Indian rugs, saddle blankets, decorative
hangings, bedspreads, serapes and r
Navajo designs, Chimayo designs, ori
Quiche Indian blankets. Handwoven by In
in Mexico and Central America.

HUGE SELECTION

(Independent and out-of-town dealers welc

FREE CATALOG: DUSTY HENSON
P.O. Box 12360, El Paso, Tx. 79912

ABOVE: More road shows,
1978 and 1979.
RIGHT: Bonnie at
a Kansas City
road show.

El Paso Saddleblanket showroom in Phoenix, Arizona, 1983.

ABOVE: *Bonnie in our Navajo Rug Gallery, Scottsdale, Arizona.*
LEFT: *We used this same photo in the newspaper ad that we ran in the* Phoenix Gazette, *1980.*

ABOVE: Bonnie and me with Ben Johnson, movie actor and star of many Westerns, at the El Paso Saddleblanket showroom in Scottsdale, Arizona, 1980. RIGHT: Red Skelton made this sketch for Bonnie while visiting our gold jewelry showroom in Scottsdale. BELOW: Steve McQueen bought rugs from us while filming in Old Tucson, 1978.

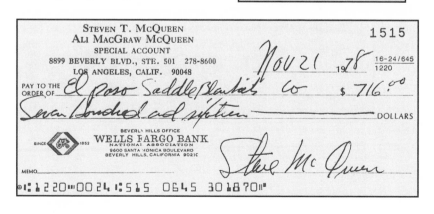

*El Paso Saddleblanket
Company's Alameda Street
warehouse, El Paso, Texas.
By the time we set up this
warehouse in 1984 we were
solidly in the cowhide business,
importing twenty percent of
Brazil's hair-on hides.*

*We mailed tens of thousands of postcards in English and Spanish in the early
'80s promoting our Alameda Street wholesale warehouse in El Paso. It was an
exciting growth period for us.*

Buying our first container of cowhides at the tannery with Herman Lorsche, our agent, Brazil, 1982. Herman passed away in 2000.

ABOVE: In 1988 we traded for this house on Pennsylvania Circle in El Paso, Texas.
RIGHT: Bonnie and me at an Americana Museum art show, El Paso, Texas, 1988.

ABOVE: I loaned one of my old Cadillacs to members of the Texas Tornados in 1989. (Left to right) Flaco Jiménez, Augie Meyer, Doug Sahm, and Freddy Fender. RIGHT: Freddy Fender joking with me about the Cadillac breakdown.

LEFT: Pete Duarte, El Paso medicine man and shaman (on left), myself, and Billy Gibbons of ZZ Top.

TOP: *Me with wallabies (kangaroos) in Australia.*
ABOVE: *Bonnie and me in Sweden, 1988.*
LEFT: *Bonnie and me in Milan, Italy, while attending Feria Milano, 1990.*

ABOVE: Bonnie and me with a rug exporter and his family on a business trip to Morroco in 1991. RIGHT: New York City, June 18, 1987. BELOW: Guatemala, 1992.

Bonnie and me in Athens, Greece.

*ABOVE: Bonnie.
LEFT: Bonnie and
me at a Samba show.
Rio de Janeiro,
Brazil, 1981.*

Election night victory party, November, 1990. (Left to right) Joe Rosson, Senator Peggy Rosson, myself and Bonnie.

Our 1957 "Campaign Cadillac" that we used in Senator Rosson's 1990 campaign.

El Paso Saddleblanket donated the "Casey Tibbs" rug at this huge Beverly Hills fundraiser in 1983, attended by many Hollywood celebrities. Among those pictured are Wilford Brimley (on far left), Casey Tibbs (fourth from left), Ben Johnson (sixth from left), Denver Pyle (third from right),and Bonnie and me (far right).

Relaxing in my El Paso office, 1991.

ABOVE: Congressman Ron Coleman, Secretary of the Treasury Lloyd Bentsen and myself, 1992.
LEFT: I met the great-great-great-grandson of Christopher Columbus at El Paso's 500 year celebration, 1992.

El Paso Saddleblanket Company's downtown warehouse
and retail outlet, El Paso, Texas 1993.

My favorite Cadillac, a '59 Limo, 1992.

Bonnie and me in El Paso Saddleblanket Company's downtown rug showroom.

Rancho El Cid, Santa Isabel, Chihuahua, Mexico

Above: View of factory buildings, Rancho El Cid, 1998.
Inset: Bonnie and me, out for a ride at Rancho El Cid, 1993.

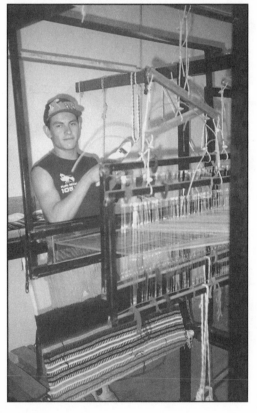

ABOVE: Some of the one hundred looms at Rancho El Cid, 1996. LEFT: A weaver at Rancho El Cid making a saddleblanket, 1995.

ABOVE: Pouring for cast iron stars at Ranch El Cid foundry. BELOW: Nick Miller, El Paso Channel 9 News Anchor, interviewing a foundry worker for his weekly "On the Road" special interest segment. Rancho El Cid, 1996.

ABOVE & RIGHT:
Mexican-style rodeo at
Rancho El Cid, 1996.

BELOW: Horseracing,
Rancho El Cid, 1995.

LEFT: We attended a reception given in our honor by the Mexican government for our helping to promote economic development. Chihuahua City, Mexico, 1997.

We sponsored the West Texas Futurity and presented awards in 1999. Also shown in photo are Hector Holguin (second from left), famous computer pioneer with his wife, Rosario (third from left) and the horse owners, trainer and jockey.

ABOVE: Bonnie and me with our dogs on the balcony of our home in El Paso, Texas. LEFT: Our house guest Billie Sol Estes, April, 2000…the legendary Texas wheeler-dealer/convicted swindler. Many people in Texas revere him as a folk hero.

"Life is good, 1996!" Bonnie and me at home standing in front of our, now famous, 1955 pink Cadillac.

Posing with "Kaw-Liga" the wooden Indian in our El Paso Saddleblanket showroom, 1999.

This upright handweaving loom is the type used to make big rugs for El Paso Saddleblanket Company, Delhi, India, 2000.

Fishing on the Rio Grande near Hillsboro, New Mexico, 2004.

SERAPES SADDLES COWHIDE

THE NEW EL PASO SADDLEBLANKET WORLD
HEADQUARTERS, EL PASO, TEXAS, *2006*

El Paso Saddleblanket World Headquarters rug showroom, 2006.

*El Paso
Saddleblanket
World Headquarters
showrooms,
2007.*

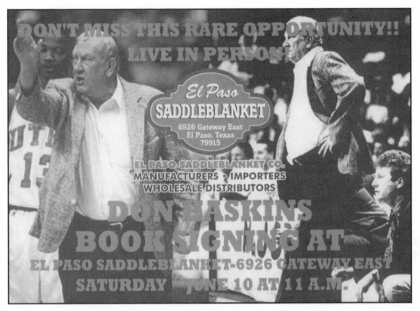

Postcard promoting the Don Haskins book signing, June 10, 2006.

Kinky Friedman book signing at El Paso Saddleblanket World Headquarters, August 21, 2006.

Above: Full page ad that appeared in color in Texas Monthly Magazine, Fall 2007. Right: We teamed up with the Tigua Pueblo Indians and had a very successful Indian Market at El Paso Saddleblanket on October 6, 2007.

PART 3
Worldwide Adventures

Chapter Fifteen

International Markets

"Forget the grammar and grace—
Dusty sure knows how to communicate."

—BONNIE HENSON

 ONE OF THE BEST THINGS about being in the import/export business is all the pre-tax dollars you can spend running around the world buying and selling. I think travel makes people more aware of what's going on in the world. We never travel just to sightsee. We travel to trade, both selling and buying. There's no more fascinating way to get to know a culture than through trade. It gives you a way to meet people, a way to deal with them, a way to get to know about their customs and their economy. And it can also make you money. What could be a better combination! Instead of coming back from a trip with a suitcase full of curios, Bonnie and I come back with contacts, names, suppliers, customers and, very often, containers full of great merchandise that we can offer to others at amazingly low prices.

We travel continuously, into the interior of Mexico sporadically and all over the world, buying up everything from rabbit skins in Spain to cattle horns in South Africa to cowhides in Brazil. The characters I've met. I tell you bro, you don't really know someone unless you've traded with them. Trade is the oldest form of human communication. Trade is older than language or politics or anything else. It's a noble profession, a tough profession and a great profession if you want to get to know people.

We traveled a lot to Mexico and Central America and across the Southwest as we established El Paso Saddleblanket. But we didn't really start to venture to other places until 1987. Bonnie can tell the story better than I can.

"In 1987, after El Paso Saddleblanket had settled in its downtown El Paso location, we launched a worldwide search for customers and products. We were already firmly established with suppliers in Mexico, Central and South America, but now we headed to the Old World. When our old travel companion, Sid the German shepherd, died there was a void in our life and fast paced travel helped.

"We've chalked up nearly a million air miles with American Airlines and a bunch more with Lufthansa, British Air and Air China. Most of our trips were for less than fourteen days, because, after a week or so, we started feeling too detached from the El Paso operation. This was before e-mail and overseas phone calls were difficult and costly."

WE TRAVELED DOWN TO BRAZIL and hooked up with a fellow named Herman Lorsche who supplied us with cowhides and sheepskins for many years until he passed away. Now his associate continues to supply us. It's always a pleasure to travel down to Brazil, go to their tannery and examine the high quality cowhides.

For a while, we were importing whips and quirts from Brazil. It was a good business, but we had some of the strangest clients ordering them. We sold one called "the cat with five tails" to some porno places in L.A.

On a trip to Brazil in 1980, we traveled up the Amazon River to Manaus. In Manaus, I met a guy from upstate New York. He had come to Manaus thirty years earlier, had married a Brazilian gal and had never been back to the states. He was running a little craftshop at the time I met him. He had some interesting items that he bought from the Brazilian Yanomami Indians: masks, baskets, and blowguns.

Well, I started buying from this fellow. After a couple of years we got to be pretty good friends, and we built up a pretty good business. We shipped the products to Guatemala, then reshipped them to the U.S. as Guatemalan handicrafts to get a special freight rate.

Anyhow, one day this old New Yorker in Manaus got into a bad car wreck and went into a coma. When he woke up, he was completely paralyzed. I called him up to see how he was doing and I said, "Hey, you gotta get better. We have business to take care of!"

The old boy knew I was kidding him along, but I think it helped him get a positive attitude towards his illness. He managed to gain enough mobility so that he could get around with a cane. He recovered and we did more business together.

OUTSIDE THE U.S., we sell to Canada, Europe, Japan and Australia. Australian people like our products pretty good but the freight is a killer, so we've never sold too much there. On the first trip I made to Australia, I traded some Mexican rugs for a bunch of "Roo" hides and boomerangs to a guy from Alice Springs (in the outback). I love the Aussie sense of humor and their seemingly carefree ways. Australia is a real party place that consumes more alcohol per capita than any other English speaking country in the world. Wow! I noticed how many people have all these great tattoos.

Canada is our biggest foreign market. To me, Canadians are a lot like us because Western Canada is like our West and Eastern Canada is more like the East. We really got along well with the French Canadians because they seem to be a lot like the Hispanic people here on the border in that they love to eat well and have a great time. We sell a little bit of everything in Canada. The people are fairly conservative when it comes to business, and they are more loyal to companies and products than us Americans.

• • •

One of the most amazing showrooms I've ever visited was outside of Oslo, Norway. A guy named Eddie owned the place. It was way out in the country, and when we arrived there I couldn't believe it. Eddie had a 3,000 square foot showroom jammed full of fur coats—minks, fox, an unbelievable assortment. And here he was, way out in the country.

"Eddie," I asked, "you've got so much inventory. Where do you sell it?"

"Retail mostly," he said.

"You don't export?"

"Oh, no…"

I couldn't believe this. "You've got so many furs in here, and you're stuck way out in the country. Who buys from you?"

"One hundred people live in this town," Eddie said. "They buy. There is another town with eighty people fifteen kilometers away. They buy…"

He mentioned two or three other little towns in the area. I couldn't believe that such a small population could support such a big fur shop. I figured that Norwegians must really like furs. To this day, we still trade Eddie Mexican-baja shirts for reindeer hides.

Communication is always a problem when you are traveling overseas. One time we had a little communication problem in France. I'll let Bonnie tell the story.

"I studied a little French in high school which seemed totally useless until we visited Paris in 1990. A taxi driver was being difficult and a real jerk. He was not taking us to the hotel we requested. Because I remembered a little bit of French, I told Dusty that the taxi driver was using the excuse that we had not given him the EXACT address—but we knew it was just two blocks from the Arc de Triumph. Dusty lost his patience, reached for the driver's shirt collar, pulled his head back and whispered to him clearly, 'OK, asshole, take us EXACTLY to the Arc de Triumph and we'll walk from there.' Amazing how that communiqué got through. All of a sudden the driver found the hotel. I learned from Dusty a long time ago that speaking correctly and communicating weren't the same. Therefore I have given up on changing Dusty's talk to proper English. Forget the grammar and grace—Dusty sure knows how to communicate."

. . .

WE TRAVELED TO MOROCCO to buy rugs. I loved the markets, the traders, and the snake charmers. Bonnie came away with her own impressions of the trip, which she recorded in a letter to her parents. Not having ever traveled much, they enjoyed seeing the world through her eyes.

"MOROCCO: *It does not matter whether or not you know that geographically it is situated in the northwest part of Africa… Think of it in your mind only as an ancient illusion… somewhere at the edge of the twilight zone.*

"Jesus and Mohammed still exist. But today they wear Rolexes and fly in Lear jets. Snake charmers do exist and are quite common in the market areas. The casual observer might not notice their presence at first, because the snakes are kept under tambourines. If you express interest in a performance, they get the vipers out from their covers.

"I am extremely uncomfortable in the presence of snakes of any kind or size. We saw great pythons in the Amazon, but they were in a deep pit. Here, the cobras were a mere ten feet away from me.

"Because Dusty truly wanted to see this attraction, I sat nervously through several minutes of haunting flute music and writhing snakes. Just when I thought the worst was over, a final tambourine was lifted to reveal a creature that appeared to be a very close relative to the rattlesnake. My worst nightmare came to life when the charmer moved closer to me and tried to put the snake in my hands.

"My entire body broke out in a cold sweat. Adrenaline surged through my heart and stomach.

"I wanted to scream.

"I wanted to run—but I was virtually paralyzed by fear. Dusty jumped in between me and the snake and quickly moved me away. That may be the last time I ever go near a tambourine.

"Later, returning to the security of the hotel room, I collected my thoughts and wrote the following poem, which can be sung to the tune of 'On Top of Old Smokey.'

> *"On top of a camel, in the desert Sahare,*
> *I lost my dear Dusty, he's out there somewhere.*

He went with the Berbers, to see the snake charm.
But they saw his Rolex, and cut off his arm.

I'm not a crybaby, I'm quite a good sport,
Just please save his blue jeans, he's got my passport!

"*About the people—have you ever seen an ant farm? Or can you imagine the way that millions of ants live in little tunnels? This is the best way I can describe the medina—the old city where the common people live. The city is entirely surrounded by thick walls with only two or three entrances. The streets are not designed for vehicles… These cities date back to the Ninth century! Some streets are about eight feet wide, some only about four feet wide. Thousands of people, some leading burros, move through these narrow corridors going about their daily routines.*

"*You never know what you will see or smell when you poke your head into a doorway. It could be a large merchant's house covered with fine tapestries, a workshop for copper or bronze smiths, or maybe a donkey stable. You see just about everything.*"

ISTANBUL is another great place for a trader. In fact, the city has been a center for trade between East and West for thousands of years. Our introduction to Istanbul came by way of a trader named Fari. Fari was a Turkish guy whose family was from Istanbul. I met him while he was living in El Paso. He was doing real well selling tapestries of the dogs playing pool and the Virgin of Guadalupe and religious stuff all over Mexico. The tapestries were made in Turkey on some kind of velvet-like fabric.

Anyway, Fari was selling container loads of this stuff. He met a lady here, got married and opened up an Oriental rug store briefly in El Paso. I bought stuff from him for years, and he bought stuff from me, and we got to be pretty good friends.

Well, one day I said to Bonnie, "Let's go find us some rugs in Turkey. I've never been there." Sure enough, we flew into Istanbul and old Fari met us at the airport. He was a great host. We had a great time visiting his yacht and eating at the restaurant his folks owned and buying lots of rugs and things and finding good deals everywhere. Of course, I'm lucky. I have a cast iron stomach. Bonnie's perspective is a little bit different. While she was stuck in the hotel room one day recovering from a touch of food poisoning, she wrote this Old World travel account in a letter to her mother.

"Now let us stare out into the beautiful harbors of Istanbul, where merchant ships have traversed the seas for centuries. No amount of reading in history books can shed a true light on the complex transitions that brought about what is today Istanbul. Seeing the city pulse at daybreak is to witness a stage of characters portraying several centuries and cultures all reading lines to each other. Some in complete understanding, others frustrated and confused.

"A smartly dressed business man parks his Mercedes across from a centuries old Byzantine mosque. He tucks his portable phone in his briefcase and struts toward a fruit stand (a horse drawn cart). The few lire received by the vendor is warmly welcomed as it is the first sale of many, many transactions he must make during a day to support himself.

"Sometimes, the farmer's wife sits near the cart quietly cleaning and spinning wool. Some even bring live sheep with them if it is necessary to sell some of the flock. The animals seem quite content to pass the day mowing down weeds on a vacant lot. No one harasses the street vendor or his animals. There seems to be great tolerance for all enterprise.

"One of the livelier centers of commerce these days is the Bulgarian Flea Market. Poor rural people, recently freed from Communism, are flocking to snatch up cheap goods they previously had no access to. The rather dowdy scarf-covered women are not purchasing items of great value, rather more utilitarian. But the enthusiasm of the shoppers rivals that of a Japanese tour bus storming Rodeo Drive. Same excitement, different income levels.

"Istanbul has not lost all the glory of its past. The architecture of the ancient mosques is still a breathtaking sight. And most are NOT hidden by modern expansion because they sit as huge fortresses on the hillsides of the Bosporus (the waterway passing through Istanbul).

"Istanbul is so huge it sits on two continents: both Europe and Asia. Some ten million people exist and trade in this enormous center of business.

"The Bazaar of Istanbul is quite an adventure. There are over four thousand stalls of vendors hawking their wares. The merchants are aggressive out of sheer necessity, but never outright rude.

"Again gazing out toward the water I see and hear a commotion of flapping wings and squawking birds. Seems the seagulls have a disagreement about fishing rights. In fact, this whole side of the world seems to be having disagreements with each other. There is such a tremendous clashing of old and new, political ties and anarchy.

"While I sit here so peacefully gazing at the ancient mosques, I am suddenly jolted back to the present when a fax is shoved under the door (an up-to-the-minute report of what's happening at El Paso Saddleblanket)."

Chapter Sixteen

The Wild, Wild East

*"After trading in foreign countries,
you realize how easy it is to deal with Americans."*

 BONNIE AND I FIGURE that over the years we have traveled to forty-nine different capital cities in Central and South America, Europe, the Middle East, Africa, Australia and Asia. Some of the wildest trips we had were in Asia. I call it the wild, wild east.

Take the Philippines for example. A huge country made of many separate islands. It's a tough place to live and a tough place to trade. I set up a deal in the Philippines to have a bunch of stuff manufactured: red chile ristra type jewelry and chile necklaces. In fact, I had a whole bunch of different chile merchandise that I had manufactured in the Philippines.

One of my contacts over there was a big trader. He lived in a building that looked like a fortress out in the middle of the jungle. It was a four-story building. He lived on the top story, and all his merchandise was stored in the floors below.

I bought a forty-foot container full of merchandise from this guy. And one of the things I bought was a bowie knife, a real big knife. What I liked about the knife was that it had a little monkey skull on the outside of the scabbard. I just bought one for a sample and packed it in the container.

So we get back to the states, and the container comes into New Orleans. I get a call from the boys at customs, "Mr. Henson, you've got this monkey head on this knife."

"Yes," I said.

"Well, we need the scientific name of the monkey."

I laughed. "Tell you what fellows, just go ahead and throw that knife away."

"No, sir. We can't do that. We need the scientific name of the monkey."

Great! My whole shipment was tied up because they needed the scientific name of a fucking monkey! It took me two weeks to find out the name of that monkey. And for part of the time the port of New Orleans was charging us drayage time. By the time I got the monkey's name, the whole operation had cost me an extra $700.

BONNIE WROTE some of her best travel letters from Asia. She wrote them down right when we were in the midst of our travels, so they give a clear impression of what we were going through as we traveled around. She wrote the following letter to her mother about traveling in Bangkok, Thailand and Manila, in the Philippines.

"We're in Bangkok, Thailand on the other side of the world. It may as well be the dark side of the moon—that's how strange and far away it seems. I remember when I went to the one-room school house near our farm in grade school. All of us kids eagerly awaited the National Geographic *to read about far off places like this. I'm not sure we realized they really existed. It was just entertainment. None of us ever dreamed we'd someday actually travel around the world.*

"Bangkok is beautiful for its architecture and landscaping. It should be a paradise, but there is a very dark side to its backstreets. It's a progressive city, where free enterprise thrives. If you don't have a good job or a good future, you can still make a lot of money by going into the streets and selling your little sister or brother to perverts, who buy them by the hour for sex. Nine to eleven-year-olds bring the best price. A little sick, yes? Yes, but it is true. I'd never mention something as horrible

as this, except that it is all over the newspapers here. The government realizes what a problem it is.

"Dusty is always interested in seeing the real 'business' side of a city. We walked miles though crowded streets and alleys, markets and red-light districts. The street traffic of both vehicles and pedestrians moving together is an unbelievable traffic jam. In a taxi it commonly takes twenty to thirty minutes to go one mile.

"One of the funniest things we did in Bangkok was to go to a restaurant called 'The Seafood Market.' Picture in your mind a combination of a fresh food grocery store combined with a full service restaurant. When you enter, you receive a grocery cart. You then go all around the edges of the building to select from the showcases your seafood, your vegetables, potatoes, bread, wine, fruit, etc. You go through a check-out stand and pay. Then you are seated at a table. A waiter comes to ask you how you would like each item to be cooked. It was amazing how efficiently they got the prepared meal back to the table. We had lobster, clams, oriental vegetables, fried potatoes and garlic bread. That was probably the best meal of the whole trip.

"In Manila, the poorest of the poor were asked to contribute money to benefit Imelda Marcos on her return. This is a woman who spent her country's money on shopping for three thousand pairs of shoes! Why do they worship this woman? I'm sorry... I don't understand. Can you imagine in Texas if the people who can't afford enough milk for their babies were asked for donations so that Governor Ann Richards could buy cigarettes? It's a reasonable comparison.

"But then, I am a visitor. I have no right to criticize those things which I do not fully understand. Only in America do we believe that every human has the right to grow, to earn, to live in peace and privacy. We are very fortunate indeed that our government cannot sell us like livestock."

BACK IN 1989 we worked our first trade show in Tokyo, Japan. We had all our business cards printed in Japanese on one side and English on the other side as is the tradition in Japan. We learned that Japanese people are not impulsive buyers like we are because we did not write one single order at the show. We knew they liked the product, but it is their custom to go very slow and have meetings before buying anything.

However, we made some contacts at the show with a few companies that placed orders some time later. And we even had a couple of groups we met over there travel to Texas to buy from us here in El Paso. I remember one Monday morning this Japanese guy came in and picked out about $10,000 worth of merchandise. The next morning we received a bank wire transfer from Japan for the full amount. Great, we thought. Then this guy came back the next day and picked out another $10,000 worth of merchandise. Sure enough, the next day we received another $10,000 wire transfer. We were really happy then. The next morning the guy picked out another $10,000 worth of merchandise and we received another $10,000 wire transfer. Then the same thing again! Anyway, this went on for five days—$50,000 worth of merchandise!

The guy spoke very broken English but was so nice and pleasant that all of us really did get to know this guy pretty well. He stayed at the International Hotel located next to us, and every night he got hammered big time at the hotel bar. He had terrible hangovers in the mornings and he got so comfortable with us after a couple days that he went back into our shipping department, curled up like a cat and took a nap on top of a pile of rugs. He was such a super guy and such a super customer that that Friday night we threw him a private party with all our employees at the hotel bar. He got pretty drunk again, but this time he wasn't the only one.

A couple years ago, Sherman Barnett, owner of Barnett Harley Davidson, calls me and says that he's sending over this stretch limo full of Japanese people. They had just spent over $500,000 with him on custom bikes. Sherm said the leader of the group owned thirty motorcycle stores in Japan, and he said, "When they come in, you won't have a difficult time picking out who's the boss."

Sure enough, the limo pulled into the parking lot. So, just for fun, I rounded up our whole staff to meet him in the parking lot. We lined up single file on both sides as he got out of the limo. We laughed and bowed and had a great time. He loved the attention and spent a few thousand with us that day. Sherman was right, there was no question who was Mr. Big.

• • •

I GOT INTO a pretty interesting art deal in China in the late 1980s. You know all those ads you see on TV—"Starving Artists' Show at the Holiday Inn, Sunday at 2 P.M.!" It always seems like they're having a "starving artist" show at two or three different locations in any town. Well, all that starving artist art is from Hong Kong. Folks in Hong Kong buy it from mainland China and ship it over here. There's no duty and no inspection of the merchandise. Why? Because it's art.

So I get an idea. Why not have Western-style paintings done in China? I went to Gallup, New Mexico. A friend there owned trading posts and sold a bunch of Indian art, cowboy art, and other Southwestern-style stuff. I went to his store with a Polaroid, and I took shots of his paintings and hit the bookstores and got lots of ideas for paintings.

I had leads on two or three places in Hong Kong. I went over there and made a fabulous deal. I contracted these people to make these paintings. Of course, we had to work out some of the details. Some of the cowboys and Indians pictures had oriental faces! After we got all the production problems solved, I then went to Tijuana, Mexico and set up a stretching machine and a frame factory.

I sold thousands of paintings over the next few years, but the business turned out to be more trouble than it was worth. At least it gave us an excuse to explore Hong Kong. Although I don't think Bonnie liked it as much as I did.

"In Hong Kong I can't stand eating in the seafood restaurants because even though the fish has been dipped in boiling water, or tossed on a grill, the tail is still flapping on the plate when the waiter puts it in front of you. This is not my idea of a good meal!

"I'm ready to get back to El Paso. The distance from home is getting to me. Just one more day of tramping through the markets, things squishing under my feet, pungent aromas, strange sounds. I didn't use the camera much, but my mind has ten thousand images."

• • •

OVER THE LAST FEW YEARS I have made several trips to India to set up production of products. Most of the products were new to our customers and included such things as coir (coconut fiber) doormats with Southwest and cowboy designs provided by us, handwoven cotton mats with our special stenciled designs, art coral necklaces and beautiful leather animal figures.

India is the only country in the world that I go to alone. Bonnie is a very experienced traveler and has certainly been exposed to many different cultures, but I'm glad I spared her from these trips. India is a huge, sprawling, turbulent, poor country and traveling there can be a grueling experience.

The first time I went, other than reading a few travel books, I had no knowledge of the country and did not know a soul in India. I noticed that Indians made many textiles with jute, a hemp-type fiber. I also reasoned that if I got into the hemp/jute business and couldn't sell it, what the hell, I could always SMOKE it!

I figured that Delhi, being the capitol, would be a great place to start looking for products. In Delhi, the population and concentration of people is mind boggling. In 1947, when India got its independence from Great Britain, the population was about 350 million. Today the population is around one billion and growing rapidly. On every rooftop, under every bridge, in the median between roads, just everywhere, everywhere I looked in India, I saw thin, hungry, homeless people. I just couldn't help thinking how much I would like to have the Jerry Falwell-type, radical pro-lifers get an eye full of this.

The bicycle rickshaw guys all had about a three or four foot diameter basket sitting on top of their bicycle, where they curled up like a cat and slept. The soiled rags of clothing they wore were their only possession, and they were completely nomadic with no home. They made enough money each day to buy a few handfuls of food and survive to the next day.

Big, ugly buffalo cattle roamed around everywhere. People rushed to claim the dung, which they dried and used for cooking fuel. Thousands of men squat in a sitting position everywhere, as they have no hope of furniture. Sometimes I saw rows of men sitting like this on a fence and it reminded me of doves sitting on a telephone line. All the sidewalks, buildings and walls were red from people chewing and spitting betel nut (a mild narcotic, not bad). Some men chewed constantly, and if they had any teeth, the betel juice turned them red.

North India is about forty percent Muslim. Most of the rest of the people are Hindu with a very, very small percentage of Christians. The Muslims are easy to spot because of their clothing and because the men have facial hair. The men you see in the movies, etc., with the turbans are Sikhs. The Sikhs follow a religion that developed from Hinduism but is now definitely on its own. Sikhs make up only a small percentage of the population, but they are a visible and successful group—engineers, military men, some merchants and clerks.

India is a very colorful country with lots of folks willing to cooperate with you on anything you need to do. Especially in the rural areas where I traveled, the poverty is unbelievable. Begging, starving people are the norm. I have seen some rough places in my life, but I was not prepared for the things I saw in India. Some of these guys made even the most hardened street hustlers in Juárez look like amateurs.

Anyway, my search for products led me to Agra and a Jain family that owned a jute rug and mat factory. The Jains people follow their own religion that is hundreds of years old. The Jain community is better off than the majority of Indian communities and is made up of, for the most part, merchants and traders. I traveled a couple of hours outside of Agra to meet this Jain family and arrived at this old, old, big warehouse and textile factory in the worst slum area you can imagine. It was actually more of a fortress. This very wealthy Jain family lived in a large apartment above the factory.

Just like the TV show "Dallas," the whole family lived together—the old father Enkay and his sons Ajay and Sanjay and their wives. They all shared the same last name: Jain. I stayed with them for three days. We designed weavings, visited their factories during the day and had lots of philosophical and religious discussions at night. Jains are vegetarians, but do not eat any vegetables that are grown under the ground such as potatoes, onions or carrots. Also Jains eat nothing between sundown and sunrise but can drink water. It was the strangest environment I've ever been in, and yet I felt extremely comfortable around my new friends.

In Mexico, our four-harness shuttle weaving looms are set up on a platform with legs like a table. In India, they build the looms flat on the ground, then dig a pit in front of the loom where the weaver stands and operates the handloom, thus saving the expense of putting legs on the looms. On my second trip to India and the jute weaving factory outside Agra, Sanjay Jain told me that, fairly recently, a big cobra had crawled into one of these pits and had bitten a weaver. Sanjay said the weaver was extremely lucky to be alive because the cobra needs to twist its head in order for the fangs to release all the venom. In this case, somehow the snake didn't give the weaver the full dose.

I started to look around my legs more carefully. Sanjay assured me, "Not to worry, Mr. Dusty, cobra comes only in Monsoon season."

"Well," I asked, "what season is it now?"

He stalled a little bit, smiled and answered, "It is monsoon season."

When we were walking through the factory he pointed to one of the weavers and said, "He dresses like a woman." Wow! A sure 'nuff cross-dressing transvestite weaver in India. I gotta say I've known and seen a lot of weavers in my day, but that was a first for me.

A couple of years ago, one of my business associates from India came to visit us in El Paso. We took him to a Mexican food restaurant. Several of our employees also joined us for lunch that day. Just for fun, I picked up a bowl of very HOT pico de gallo sauce from the center of the table and said, "Here, eat this soup." We all watched and waited for his reaction. His eyes turned red, but to our surprise he said, "Oh, yes, I like this very, very much. But in India we like it even MORE spicy."

I learned a lot about India from my Jain friends and enjoyed hearing their philosophies of life. My stories about life on the Mexican border seemed to fascinate them. We still do business and I communicate with them regularly via e-mail.

Chapter Seventeen

Politics is Good Business

"I'm a fiscal conservative but social liberal.
Boy, I believe in everything. Pro-choice, pro-everything.
I'm not a Republican or a Democrat."

TRAVEL IS A GREAT WAY of finding out what's going on in the world. Politics is a great way of finding out what's going on at home. And El Paso, Texas has some of the most interesting politics in the world and has had for some time. Back in the 1880s, Wyatt Earp visited El Paso, spent one night and left the next day for Tombstone, Arizona. He thought El Paso was too dangerous.

Politics anywhere is more than a hobby. It's good business. Being active in politics helps us stay in touch with the decision makers in our community. It helps our business maintain a high profile, and it gives us the financial contacts that we need as our business grows and expands.

I wasn't always interested in politics. I've never been one to get involved with groups, organizations or causes. In my mind I was a self-proclaimed citizen of the world who took the global view. To me, it always seemed more important whether Pakistan nuked India, or if the exchange rate of the Brazilian *cruzeiro* dropped against the U.S. dollar than who won the city council seat in my district.

Over the years there have been a few candidates who came by our showroom soliciting campaign donations, but that was pretty much the extent of our involvement. I'd cough up a fifty-dollar bill or something, the money and the candidate would disappear about as fast as a piece of fried chicken around our German shepherds, and that would be that.

We remained indifferent to politics until 1989 when Bonnie and I met Peggy Rosson at a friend's Christmas party. She was running for the Texas Senate at the time. Our involvement in her campaign and the friendship that we developed changed my life and views forever.

THE MOST IMPORTANT RULE I've learned in politics is this: don't make enemies, make friends. Of course, politics is a tough business and sometimes it's hard to keep smiling. But I always try. I honestly do.

The other rule in politics is that if you zing somebody, they're going to zing you back. In other words, if someone does you a favor or gives you money, you will eventually have to do a favor for them. There's a balance sheet in politics just like there is in business. And in both business and politics, there's no such thing as a free lunch.

But just because lunch ain't free don't mean it ain't fun! The great thing about living, working and being involved in El Paso politics is the chance I've had to meet so many great local people over the years.

Take, for instance, Mr. Jonathan Rogers. He was probably the most influential man in El Paso and did as much or more than any other person to help El Paso grow and prosper. He was one of a kind. He usually prefered to stay behind the scenes, but when he decided he'd had enough of something, he was not shy about stepping up and fixing it. In one such example, in the early 1980s he jumped into politics and ended up serving four terms as our mayor. He died in 2007 after a brief illness.

In the late 1980s, when the banking crisis hit and banks were being sold and merged almost every week, Rogers watched as a number of national chain banks came into El Paso and took more and more of El Paso's capital out of the community. He didn't like what he saw, so he fixed it. He, John MacGuire, and several others decided to form a local bank dedicated to serving El Pasoans and keeping their money in El Paso.

In 1990, I was honored when Mr. Rogers offered me the opportunity to be one of the original investors in Bank of the West. I don't look like a banker, but Mr. Rogers knew me and knew my business. That's one of the great things about El Paso. People here on the border don't care about history or lineage. They are very accepting and take you for what you are. And with Bonnie and me, what you see is what you get. Now the original bank in downtown has grown into five banks across the city and the stock has skyrocketed.

Another great El Pasoan that I've gotten to know through politics is Mike Dipp. Mike's family migrated from Lebanon to Guadalajara, Mexico, then his father settled in El Paso. Mike is in the wholesale grocery business, among other things. He is one of the most generous and civic-minded individuals I have ever met. Mike has helped hundreds of people in hundreds of ways and is involved in almost every political race in town. I always like to hear Mike quote car-maker Henry Ford, "Never complain, never explain."

Mike once paid me a great compliment. "Dusty," he said, "your house is the Switzerland of El Paso. Everyone from all parts of town can get together at your house, relax, talk and start to work things out."

I've OPENED UP MY HOUSE to politicians of all kinds. I enjoy knowing and working with people who have different political views. Democrats, Republicans, it really doesn't matter to me, as long as I think the person is honest and will work for the good of El Paso.

I've thrown parties for candidates from constable to senator. One of the biggest parties I ever threw was for our old friend, Alicia Chacon. I set up a mariachi band on the roof of our pool house, a rock band on the balcony of the house, a piano player in the living room and had dancers from Juárez performing on the patio. We filled the fountain with 1,500 pounds of ice and beer and had waiters and bartenders circulating all through the house. The place was packed with about six hundred people. It wasn't cheap and afterwards the whole neighborhood was littered with our red plastic cups. But it was a helluva party, and Alicia won the election!

As I MENTIONED, it was Peggy Rosson's campaign for State Senator that really began our involvement in politics. When we met, we immediately liked her. After we talked for a while, it was pretty clear that she was smart, open and direct, but at the same time she was so soft-spoken and seemed so shy that she was about the unlikeliest candidate we'd ever run across.

She wasn't new to politics. In fact she had a pretty interesting background, but this was her first run for office. She had worked as a paralegal for years, retired to become a full-time wife, later offered to do volunteer work for the city and was appointed to the El Paso Utility Regulatory Board. She became a respected authority on utility regulation and chaired the Board from 1978 to 1983. She was also active in the Democratic Party, serving as precinct chair and volunteering on numerous campaigns, including Mark White's bid for governor. Utility rates and nuke plant cost overruns were big issues in White's campaign. When his opponent, Governor William Clements, was asked during an interview whether he would appoint a consumer to the Public Utility Commission of Texas, he responded that there were no "housewives" in Texas qualified to serve on the PUC! White quickly responded that there were and that if elected, he would appoint one. Mark White won and kept his promise by appointing Peggy as the first woman to serve on and chair the Commission.

A LOT OF THINGS WERE CHANGING in El Paso in 1990 and many people felt that one thing that needed changing was our senator. He had served in the Senate for eighteen years and in the House for a long time before that. An incumbent with that many years in office is hard to beat and nobody had been willing to challenge him for years. Besides his incumbency, there were a few other things that Peggy would have to overcome: in a community that was seventy-two percent Hispanic, he spoke Spanish and she didn't. He was charming. She was sincere. He was funny. She was as "serious as a heart attack." He was warm and quick with a hug. She was shy and came across as cool and aloof. It was going to be a tough, uphill battle.

What a challenge! We decided we would do everything we could to get her elected!

SENATOR ROSSON has agreed to tell you a little about the campaign from her perspective:

"As I'm sure you've noticed, when Dusty and Bonnie decide to do something, they don't hold back. Meeting them was undoubtedly one of the best things that's ever happened to me, period. But meeting them when I did and having them with me during my campaign was nothing short of a miracle!

"As Dusty has mentioned, we met at a party and clicked. Maybe it was because Bonnie and I had the same midwestern roots and common sense way of looking at things, or because my politics meshed with theirs. Or maybe my campaign situation reminded them of the kinds of challenges they had to overcome when they first started out in their pick-up truck.

"I had a really great, if tiny, team of talented, dedicated people working on my campaign. I had a lot of quiet, underground help from people who couldn't afford to offend the incumbent and up-front help from the El Paso New Car Dealers Association, who called a press conference, said it was time for a change and that they were behind me. (This despite the anguished screams of their state association and lobbyist who knew how much punishment it could cost them if I lost!)

"I had a great logo and incredible name recognition. What I didn't have was the ability to easily walk into a room full of strangers, stick out my hand and ask for their vote! One of the first things Dusty did was give me a book called How To Work A Room. *I read it, but it didn't take. I went to candidate school. No help. I went to a communications expert. No help. I was never going to pass 'Chit-chat 101.' I was never going to master the art of being asked one question but answering a different one of my choosing, and I was never going to master the so-called Pat, Shake & Go: smile, say howdy-do, pat the back, pump the hand and move on to the next person, all in fifteen seconds. I'd smile, a person would ask me*

a question or want to voice a gripe and I'd spend the next fifteen minutes with them! You don't meet many people that way. Time was getting short! It was January and the Democratic primary was set for early March.

"On top of all my personal shortcomings, the press had characterized my supporters as a ragtag band of volunteers out scrounging for $100 donations, while thousands upon thousands of lobby dollars poured in for my opponent. Dusty to the rescue! My campaign colors were red, black and white. Out of nowhere black T-shirts materialized with 'ROSSON'S RAGTAGS' emblazoned on them. A real morale buster had been turned into a badge of honor!

"The next thing I knew, Dusty's in-store weaver had made a big rug with my name on it, the rug was draped across the back of Bonnie's vintage Ford convertible, and Dusty had somehow persuaded his good friend, actor Richard Farnsworth, that the fun way to spend a cold and windy El Paso afternoon would be to ride with us in the Rodeo Parade!

"After that the marketing wizard really shifted into high gear. One day Dusty called and asked us to come down to the store. My husband Joe and I pulled into the Saddleblanket parking lot and damn near fell out of the car. There sat one of Dusty's Cadillacs, a beautiful, black 1957 Coupe de Ville, with PEGGY ROSSON FOR STATE SENATOR very professionally painted on the sides. I was stunned!"

I DROVE PEGGY in that Cadillac all over El Paso. Even when we weren't driving it, it was working for us. Bonnie and I parked it all over town where it was sure to be noticed. One time I parked it by mistake in a lot that was owned by folks who were opposed to Peggy. Sure enough, they had it towed.

But that didn't stop us. Peggy might have been shy, but I sure wasn't. I started taking her to every event I could think of, leading the charge through the crowd. It didn't matter to me if she was tired or had a toothache or anything else. I made sure that Peggy shook hands with as many voters as possible, sometimes twice!

We even used some hook items from El Paso Saddleblanket in the campaign. One of the most popular was worry dolls from Guatemala.

The legend was that if you told your worries to the dolls and stuck them under your pillow, they would worry for you and you could get a good night's sleep. Peggy would tell people that she would worry about their problems for them when she was elected but, until then, they could use the dolls. The older women loved the dolls and word spread through the senior citizens' centers. One day I got a frantic call from Peggy. She had gone to a center to speak, but didn't have any dolls with her. The ladies were furious! We got a box of dolls over to her pronto, she handed them out and the ladies then sat down and listened to her.

The incumbent outspent us five to one. A few days before the election one of the newspapers reported that their polling showed him winning by eight to one. They were wrong! Peggy won with sixty-seven percent of the vote!

EL PASO HAD ALWAYS BEEN such a Democratic stronghold that if you won the primary, people took it for granted that you were the next officeholder. We had one small problem with that. Peggy had a Republican opponent! Now in politics there's two ways to run: scared or unopposed. So we kept working all through the summer and fall to keep up interest in her campaign. We had hundreds of T-shirts and baseball caps printed and got them out to supporters and kept the "Peggy car" visible all over town.

"Dusty's Cadillac turned out to be my best ambassador. I'd be out on the campaign trail and as soon as I introduced myself, the person would say 'Oh, the lady with the car!' and smile.

"Dusty and Bonnie continued to set up events and help me in every way they could. I had gotten a little more relaxed about campaigning after the primary, but there were still times when Dusty could tell I needed a good shove to get me moving and he wasn't shy about delivering it!"

Election day finally rolled around. Peggy won by more than two to one. It was one of my proudest moments. We drove the Cadillac down to the election party at Democratic Headquarters. I immediately took out a can of black spray paint and painted out the word "for" so that the logo read "PEGGY ROSSON STATE SENATOR."

Bonnie and I went down to Austin for Peggy's swearing in and stayed in close touch during the legislative session. I became her eyes and ears in El Paso and somehow ended up being her unofficial go-to-guy. A lot of people aren't comfortable contacting an officeholder directly and so they "go-to" one of their friends instead.

Shortly after Peggy took office I sent her a big velvet Elvis painting to hang in her office in the capitol. It started out as sort of a joke. Here were the other senators with big expensive paintings and artwork in their offices, some on loan from galleries, some that they owned. And there was Peggy with a velvet Elvis from Juárez! But Elvis turned out to be a real ice breaker for her and her staff.

"At first, my receptionist would see the door open a crack and then hear a whispered 'See, I told you so.' Then one-by-one staff members from other senate offices started coming by and asking if I could possibly get an Elvis for them. Pretty soon we were getting regular deliveries from Dusty and giving them away as fast as we could get them. What was commonplace in El Paso turned out to be a real hot item in Austin. At Christmas I was asked if I could get a really big Elvis for the main door prize at the Senate Staff Party. As always, Dusty delivered."

NOT ALL OF THE PARTIES we threw for politicians went smoothly. The year Peggy took office, the Lieutenant Governor formed the International Relations Trade and Technology Committee to address issues relating to the Border. Senator Carlos Truan was named Chair. Since she represented a border district, Peggy was appointed to the committee. During the interims between legislative sessions, Senator Truan held hearings all along the border on various issues, including how Texas was going to be affected by NAFTA and what Texas needed to be doing to insure that it worked to our advantage.

One of the hearings was to be held in El Paso and Bonnie and I decided to host a reception for the visiting senators. We invited all the big players to come, got to know the committee members and talk to them about their concerns. We had a really good turnout. It wasn't the usual huge, noisy crowd, but there were groups scattered all over the house, talking and getting acquainted.

Bonnie is a great piano player and there were a bunch of people in the living room listening to her play our baby grand. I was enjoying the music and the people. Then all of our full grown German shepherds started to get into it: growling, snapping and yipping at each other. Dogs are a lot like kids. They always seem to act their worst when company is around.

I stepped in between the dogs to try to calm them and one of them nipped my finger. It wasn't anything serious, but the blood began to flow from that little cut and my white shirt was soon really spattered with blood. The dogs were barking, the blood was flowing, the guests were wide-eyed with concern for their safety and mine, and Bonnie just kept right on playing the piano. The whole thing looked like a saloon fight in a western movie! Welcome to the wild, wild West, Senators! We must not have scared them too much though. Later, both the Senate and the House of Representatives passed resolutions honoring El Paso Saddleblanket for promoting international trade.

IN TEXAS, the Lieutenant Governor is the most powerful person in state government because he's also the President of the Senate. As such, he controls the fate of every piece of legislation filed. Bob Bullock took office as Lieutenant Governor at the same time Peggy joined the Senate. He was already a legend in Texas politics and probably knew more about Texas than anyone alive. His devotion to Texas was absolute and it was his habit to always close his remarks with "God Bless Texas." While Peggy said it was a very sincere prayer, there were others who quipped that it was more like a direct order. Either way, it was his trademark.

We often made customized saddleblankets for our customers and one Christmas Peggy asked us to make one for Lieutenant Governor Bullock. She wanted us to put "God Bless Texas" and "Bob Bullock" on the wear leathers. No problem! Big problem! For some reason our leather guy couldn't get the right "x"! He finally tracked one down and we got the blanket to Peggy in time for her to give it to the Lieutenant Governor for Christmas. She said he really liked it. By that time, Bonnie and I were devout fans of Lieutenant Governor Bullock and we decided to make a special limited edition of "Bob Bullock—God Bless Texas" saddleblankets. We sent him a good supply to give to his friends. In return he sent us an engraved gavel which is today on my office desk and is one of our most cherished possessions.

It was a sad day and a big loss for Texas when Bob Bullock passed away. We will never forget him.

WHEN PEGGY TOOK OFFICE in 1990, the census had been completed and it was redistricting time. New legislative districts were drawn and adopted by the legislature. Although the usual senate term is four years, after redistricting every senator had to run for office, then draw lots for two and four year terms. That way only half the Senate would be up for re-election every two years until the next census.

When Peggy got home after her first regular session and a couple of special sessions, she found that she would have two opponents in the Democratic Primary. We were off and running again! It was another hard campaign, but this time we had a little more money in the war chest and Peggy had a good record to run on. She won the primary with fifty-seven percent of the vote and had no Republican opponent. In 1993 she drew a four year term and we all heaved a sigh of relief. Then the courts overturned the redistricting plan and everybody had to run again in 1994. That time she drew no opposition.

Peggy retired from the Senate in 1997. Bonnie and I thought about selling the Cadillac but by then it had been "the Peggy car" for so long that we just gave it to Peggy and Joe as a retirement present.

"There is no way I'll ever be able to thank Dusty and Bonnie for everything they did to get me to the Senate and help me stay there. They opened their hearts, their home and their checkbook to me when it really mattered and never asked anything in return. They had skills and contacts I didn't and used them unsparingly on my behalf. When things got ugly, as they often do in politics, they hung

tough and always had my back. They shared their laughter and enthusiasm with me when I needed it the most. They were always there for me and they still are. They are family."

WORKING ON PEGGY'S CAMPAIGNS taught me a lot about what a circus and sewer politics can be sometimes, but it also taught me that there are some politicians you can trust. We made a lot of new friends, gained recognition for our company and had a lot of fun. But the real satisfaction came from helping to give a good, honest, hardworking person the opportunity to serve the people of El Paso. I'm proud of that and today Peggy Rosson remains one of my most trusted friends.

Chapter Eighteen

Rancho El Cid

"Anything worth doing is worth overdoing."

IN THE EARLY 1990S, American politics got a little too crazy for Bonnie and me. We felt like we couldn't operate any more without getting sued. El Paso had become the center for a large number of sleazy lawyers known as "sewing lawyers" for all the suits they filed against local clothing manufacturers. In 1992, for example, one out of every four of the workers at a major El Paso clothing manufacturer was collecting workman's compensation but not working. The company was going broke trying to operate in El Paso, and we didn't want to be the next victim.

With nearly fifty employees and hundreds of retail customers in and out every day, we felt vulnerable both because of lawsuits and because of government overregulation. We figured if the government was going to tax us to death and dictate every detail of running our business, why not move? And when Hillary Clinton's husband was elected president in 1992, that was it for us. Bonnie and I were both convinced that the country was in an immediate tailspin in the hands of left-wing socialist radicals. We wanted to keep the business going because it was extremely lucrative at that time but, at the same time, we wanted to keep an eye on the back door. So we decided to move to Mexico and start our business south of the border.

It wasn't only that we wanted to get away from the lawyers, politicians, and the anti-business climate in the U.S. By this time, we felt like we were losing a little of our identity in the marketplace. We really needed to get back in touch with Mexico and to give our business a public relations boost.

We also saw Mexico on the rise and America on the decline. Mexico seemed to me a place where a person could live much more by the code of the West, with the freedom to trade and do business. The economy in the Mexican state of Chihuahua, the state just south of El Paso, was booming. NAFTA was building consumers and a thriving middle class in Mexico. We realized that Mexicans had enough disposable income to eventually become important customers and that Chihuahua City was a great emerging market for El Paso Saddleblanket.

WE EXPLORED the state of Chihuahua, looking for a place to settle. About 230 miles south of El Paso and about thirty-five miles west of Chihuahua City, we found the little town of Santa Isabel. It was a nice, clean, quiet town of about two hundred people. The town is built on a big freshwater spring. In the summer, the town even had a water park with swimming pools and slides that drew visitors from Chihuahua City.

Just outside of Santa Isabel on the Santa Isabel River, Bonnie and I found a place that seemed perfect. It was a large spread with an eighty-year-old ranch house, a lake and a year-round flowing river. It was called Rancho Casa Blanca. We bought the place and renamed it Rancho El Cid, in honor of our new German shepherd puppy, Sid II, or El Cid.

Of course, buying a ranch in Mexico wasn't that easy. It took long, drawn out negotiations, but we finally sealed the deal. Then the work really began. The adobe walls of the old ranch house were still standing. Some of them were about two feet thick. The old roof beams were still there, but about half the roof was completely caved in. There was a little bit of the roof over the kitchen and the wood stove. Our first job was to rebuild the old ranch house so that we would have a place to live.

We hired a contractor to oversee construction, a Mexican-American named Mario Cobos. He was a construction guy, pretty smart and a good country boy from Marfa, Texas. Mario was fluent in Spanish and English and had done a lot of work on our house in El Paso. We got a cement mixer and a bunch of other equipment, and things went pretty well building up the place. Mario got along real well with all the local people and began to hire folks to work. He was a fighter and kind of a hell raiser, a macho guy who could get respect.

The roof on our ranch house was really funky. The people who had owned the place had put a little dirt on the top of it and a little tar each year to seal the leaks. So it was basically a tin roof with about six to eight inches of dirt and tar on it. Right next door to the ranch, some Franciscan fathers were building a *capilla*, a monument and a church dedicated to a local folk hero, Padre Maldonado. The fathers at the church needed fill dirt and we needed to haul the dirt from the roof somewhere, so we started giving the dirt to them. The fathers called it the first miracle of the *capilla*. I thought it was more of a lucky coincidence, but I had to respect their beliefs.

We wanted to get to know the people in the local area, so we donated some sacks of cement to the local school. Later I brought down a bunch of equipment for the school that a private school in El Paso had donated —desks, lamps, even old computers that had never been taken from the box. We brought down sacks full of baseball hats and T-shirts with the El Paso Saddleblanket logo on them. Mario rode his horse all over town throwing hats and shirts out to the kids and everyone else he saw. The local people got to know about us pretty quick.

It didn't take long until we knew Paco Chavez, the mayor of Santa Isabel. Shortly afterwards I invited him to El Paso and introduced him to Suzie Azar, who was the mayor of El Paso. Then he invited the mayor of El Paso to come down to Santa Isabel. Santa Isabel threw a party for Mayor Azar. Mayor Chavez even told her she could land her private plane on the highway if she wanted. The mayor of Santa Isabel was on cloud nine. He was a politician and glad to make contacts across the border. We had no problem borrowing the public city equipment from time to time for private work down on the ranch, and he became a staunch supporter of El Cid.

Soon we knew the judge, the tax collector, the local police, the city council people, the merchants and the other folks in town. It was only natural. We were the biggest employer in Santa Isabel when we had six guys working a cement mixer. Eventually, we had two hundred employees working for us in and around Santa Isabel.

OUR LITTLE TOWN actually had two names: General Trias, Chihuahua, named for a military hero, and Santa Isabel, Chihuahua. For some reason, a few Mexican towns have two names, but the local folks prefer Santa Isabel.

About three hundred people live in and around Santa Isabel. The town itself consists of *centro*, the central district, with about fifteen various businesses, and about ten *barrios*, neighborhoods. Our ranch was about a half-mile down a dirt road from centro and adjoined the Boquilla barrio, which consisted of about twenty houses. Boquilla referred to the mouth of the river, since both our ranch and the barrio were on a river. Many of the same families had lived in the same barrios for generations, and each barrio had its share of characters and its own identity. For example, the Ranchito barrio across the river from us had the reputation of being the lazy barrio, while our barrio was known for the small gang of tough country cousins from the Macias family. We hired them, and they became some of our best weavers. They proudly called themselves The El Cid Army.

Our barrio was also known for Doña Julia. She was a bootlegger and ran an operation where everybody could buy beer and tequila after hours. Old cowboys tied their horses out front and hung out at her cantina, which was also her living room. She was born in that house about seventy-five years before. She was known to gossip and became our insider on what was going on in Santa Isabel.

We were proud of the fact that Mayor Paco Chavez of Santa Isabel praised our operation in his annual state-of-the-city address. He noted the fact that we hired a mix of people from various barrios, which allowed folks to mix and get to know each other better. Some of these groups had had long-running feuds, like the Hatfields and McCoys, before they came to work at Rancho El Cid.

ONE OF THE GREAT THINGS about the ranch was that it was only a forty-minute drive from Chihuahua City, a city with McDonald's, Kentucky Fried Chicken, movie theaters, great restaurants, night clubs, cowboy beer bars and all the other comforts of home. Chihuahua City, population 600,000, was just as clean or cleaner than El Paso.

Throughout that first year we were having a blast building our facility. We built stables and cleared pastures and we entertained. Boy, did we ever entertain. It's hard for Americans to understand just how much land means to the Mexican people. Being a *don*, a landowner, and a landowner who was creating jobs, put us on a high social plane, not only in Santa Isabel but in Chihuahua City as well.

Instead of a barbecue pit, Mexicans cook out on something they call a *disco*. It's actually a plow disc with three legs that is placed over the fire and cooks in the same way as a wok. You put meat on the disco along with onions, potatoes, tomatoes, and jalapeños, and place tortillas around the edges. If the disco gets too hot, you move it from the fire. It's a great way to cook. You just grab what you want from the disco and wrap it in a flour tortilla. There are no dishes to wash. We later manufactured discos at El Cid and exported them to the U.S.

Parties in Santa Isabel are usually guy parties. The guys get together with the other guys to drink, eat and sing songs. The women kind of stay home. This was a bit of a social problem for us, because Bonnie couldn't be a big part of things, but we managed.

• • •

A LITTLE BIT ABOUT JUSTICE in Santa Isabel. I always liked the way the local police handled things. It was a lot like justice in the Old West. If you caught a person breaking into your home, it was expected that you would shoot them. If someone was caught stealing livestock, they were in big-time trouble, believe me.

Getting services in Santa Isabel was more difficult than making friends. It took us two years to get a telephone, and I paid through the nose for that. We ran on city water which ran out about two o'clock in the afternoon. Electricity went on and off. We ran on propane, which was tough to get. As difficult as it was to set up the ranch, I never paid a bribe to the local police or anyone else in Santa Isabel. I was just flat stubborn that way. Whenever I was faced with a situation, I told the fellows, "You know, I'm a friend. I'm here creating jobs for Santa Isabel. I am really sorry that we have a misunderstanding, but I'm sure that we can work everything out if we take our time and go to court." They always understood.

THE CHARACTERS IN SANTA ISABEL also made it seem like the Old West. One old cowboy hung around town. Everyone called him *Tío Viejo,* Old Uncle. He was too proud to beg, but he used to stand on the street, staring down at five or six pesos in his hand. He'd stand there and mumble to himself, "If I just had a few more pesos, I could get to Chihuahua..." So when folks passed by they just dropped a couple of pesos in his hand.

Then there was a lady who looked like an old witch and lived up in an abandoned house in a little canyon near the Boquilla. She was probably fifty or so, and she was always running around looking for her daughter. The strange thing was, she actually didn't have any daughters. But at one time she was said to be one of the most beautiful, sophisticated young ladies in this town. She had never been married. She never had any children. Her boyfriend disappeared, and she went crazy. Everyone knew her in the village. When she came into town, everyone would say, "Come on, come on over here," and they'd give her a few pesos or tortillas or some food.

Peddlers came down the road all the time selling things—milk, vegetables, motor oil, even furniture on the installment plan. All kinds of other characters dropped by the ranch: photographers, evangelists, Tarahumara Indians walking up and down the river and even saddle tramps, old broke down cowboys on horseback with their bedrolls, looking for ranch work. It was just like the Old West.

WHEN I STARTED TALKING about the idea of building a manufacturing facility, the Chihuahua state government went out of its way to help me. Bonnie and I both received official FM3 Mexican passports and immigrant status in Mexico. We set up a Mexican company, El Paso Saddleblanket De Mexico, S. A. de C.V. And we got started setting up a centralized production base and a training facility for apprentices to learn the business. We constructed our first warehouse, a dormitory and an apartment house. Mario started hiring some people to train as weavers.

Our operation had a big impact on Santa Isabel.

The government helped us out any way they could. They helped set up training programs and even tried to start a program to reintroduce sheep to the area to provide wool for weaving. We imported top quality wool from the carpet mills in Georgia and South Carolina and set up phase one—sixty first-class metal looms, which had never been set up before in Mexico. Phase two eventually brought in an additional sixty looms. They were specially designed by Mario to use spring action, something we had never seen before. We trained the workers at the ranch to handweave the top quality wool into top quality saddleblankets. We brought in *maestros*, master weavers from Oaxaca, Saltillo and Guanajuato, to teach. We got government grants to help with the program and tons of great press in the Chihuahua newspapers.

A weaving operation isn't a simple thing to set up. In addition to hiring weavers, we hired people to make the warp (the set of yarns placed lengthwise in the loom). We hired people to put the warps on the loom. We hired people to take the finished rugs off the loom, and we contracted with people to finish the weaving, to sew tags on the rugs and pack them. It was a big operation.

The weaving didn't go all that smoothly. The people of Chihuahua are farmers and ranchers who have little experience making handicrafts. One day we had a walkout. One of the weavers didn't get what she wanted and they all walked out. We kind of faced them down. "Fine," I told them. "We can get more weavers." We gave them a chance to save face and they came back. We never had any more trouble after that.

After some time, I realized that I was not particularly good at manufacturing. You have to be pretty hard-minded and efficient to be a manufacturer. I'm not a detail man. I like working from my instincts and not from my balance sheet. As we looked over our operations in Santa Isabel, we realized that the money was just not right. Our expenses were too high, and our prices were too low.

After two years of weaving and not making money, we looked around for other opportunities. We opened up a couple of satellite weaving operations in the nearby villages of Satavo and Riva Palacio. We set up a kachina doll factory in El Charco. We created a small factory on Rancho El Cid for making rustic horseshoe hangers and plaques. We had people making ladders, cleaning cow skulls, making *bully bags* (bags made out of bull scrotums) and constructing slingshots. At one time, we had about two hundred people working for us. We were the biggest employers in Santa Isabel by far. And unlike other Mexican companies, we were paying good wages and conducting all our business above board. It was a tough struggle to make it work.

ALTHOUGH BUSINESS WAS TOUGH, we still had a good time. We had our own El Cid soccer and baseball teams that competed with teams from other barrios and neighboring towns. The police soccer team usually won. We held horse races down by the river. On the day of the race, a huge crowd showed up. Our horse Chepe (short for Chihuahua Pacific locomotive) raced against Bolivar, the fastest horse in Santa Isabel. We lost.

Our barrio, Boquilla, consisted of many small houses on one or two acres of land. Most of the folks in our barrio raised a few animals and grew corn, beans and kept a vegetable garden. A river that was fed by mountain springs ran through our neighborhood. A dirt road led from the neighborhood to the centro, about a half mile away.

I noticed that this dirt road was getting kind of trashed out with beer cans and paper and plastic bags stuck in the trees and bushes. A few weeks before, I'd been visiting at Lake Chapala near Guadalajara. The lake had been choked with plants, so the citizens started a program and hired young teenagers to clean up the lake and the roads in the area. Work four hours, earn $5. That was the deal. The program worked like a charm. It was good for the kids, it cleaned up the lake, and it gave the community a sense of pride. I decided to start a program like this in our barrio. I called it *Dia del Orgullo*—Boquilla Pride Day. We talked with the local priests and told them that we would hire about twenty teenagers to clean up the river. We offered $5 and a free lunch. The fathers agreed to help spread the word. We told them that the kids should meet us at 9 A.M. We figured maybe a couple dozen kids would show up, and we'd all have a good time cleaning up the river and the dirt road to the ranch.

Well, Pride Day came around. I woke up and noticed a big crowd next door at the *capilla*. "Hmmm," I thought. "Somebody must be getting married." Then as the morning went on, the crowd kept getting bigger and bigger. By 9 A.M., there were several hundred people gathered, and I was in a panic. All those people had shown up to help with Boquilla Pride Day! Being a savvy politician, Mayor Chavez had even jumped on the Pride Day bandwagon. He had sent out the city workers, the entire police force and the city's only garbage truck.

I told the fathers, "Look, there's no way I can pay all these people."

They said, "We know, we know. They have just come to volunteer."

OK. They all didn't have to be paid, but I knew that everyone had to be fed. So we started the crowd off cleaning the river, then we went into Santa Isabel. Man, we bought every scrap of food in town and brought it back to the ranch. By the end of the afternoon, the river and the road were beautifully clean, and everyone was eating a great lunch, cooked outside on our discos. The whole thing worked out great. Pride Day is now an annual event in Boquilla—the second Saturday in October every year.

• • •

"Rancho El Cid allowed me to have a second childhood," Bonnie recalled. "Riding big, fast horses, playing with my dogs, gardening—it was the first country living I had done since growing up on the farm in Iowa. My petting zoo was a big hit with visitors—especially when the employees from El Paso brought their kids. We had a baby Brahma bull, a bighorn sheep, fifty rabbits, six goats, chickens and Dusty's favorite pets—the donkeys.

"Cooking outside was great too. Dusty's experience working at his Dad's resort helped me turn cooking for two into cooking for a crowd. We had some great barbecues. Our Chihuahua City friends loved to come out for a weekend getaway. We had three guest houses for visitors and entertained our family, Senator Rosson, Pete Duarte (the head of Thomason Hospital in El Paso) and other good friends.

"It was a fun and chaotic environment, especially on the second and fourth Friday when I would cook lunch for the staff of more than 150. I introduced them to Sloppy Joes, American-style Thanksgiving turkey and real El Paso-style Mexican food which was even hotter than they were used to in Mexico. It was hard work but I always loved life at the ranch."

ONE OF THE BEST TIMES we had at the ranch was the time we hosted a trade mission called Vecinos 2000. Through the El Paso Hispanic Chamber of Commerce we invited a hundred El Paso business people. Working with Fomento Economico we invited three hundred Mexican business people. My friend Senator Rosson and a large group of El Paso politicians and business people attended, as well as other dignitaries including our new friends Enrique C. Terraza, Chihuahua director of economic promotions, and Mayor Chavez of Santa Isabel.

Everyone got along great. We had discussions, food and sixty booths set up to show products. We even held a Mexican-style rodeo. There were *charros* as far as you could see in white hats, talking, laughing, drinking and watching the events. One of my favorite events was the *coladera*. In this event, the charro grabs a steer by the tail and twists it until he brings the steer down. It's kind of like bulldogging, but from the rear end.

The fiesta wasn't held just for trade. It was my fiftieth birthday party as well. I was feeling pretty good, and I decided that I would celebrate my birthday by riding a bull. Everyone, including Bonnie, was astounded to see me climb on the back of that two thousand pound critter. But I did it. It wasn't the longest ride in the world. In fact, it was one of the shortest. But everyone, especially the Santa Isabel locals, loved it.

IN 1996 AND 1997, we started having problems getting yarn and struggled to find new businesses for our workers. We set up a small foundry to make cast iron bells, outdoor furniture, branding irons and other products from recycled motor blocks. We had never been in the foundry business before. We soon realized that is was tricky, expensive and dangerous. Bonnie couldn't stand to watch our workers as they poured the fiery, molten metal into the molds. It was so dangerous. We finally gave up the foundry because we realized that we could buy the same objects at a good price from our Mennonite neighbors in Chihuahua who knew what they were doing.

We started another business, buying up Mexican cowboy antiques. I put the word out to all the locals that we would be buying antiques three mornings a week: Tuesday, Wednesday and Thursday. I was amazed to see the line of trucks bringing in merchandise from the bush. We expanded our search for antiques and hired kids in Chihuahua City to hand out lists of things we wanted with set prices and to tell people *"Americano compra, Americano compra..."* American buying, American buying. And we *were* buying—wagon wheels, canteens, saddles, spurs, branding irons, chaps and horseshoes.

We were buying so much that I hired pickers to work for me. They took kids from Chihuahua City and drove them to the little villages in the countryside. The kids circled through the village, knocking on doors and telling people to bring what they wanted to sell to the town plaza. I was paying good prices. I paid more that I needed to because I wanted the supply and I didn't want anyone competing against me. One of my best customers was the Brinker restaurant chain in Dallas. Brinker owns a number of famous restaurant chains including Chili's. They used the ranch antiques as decoration in their restaurants. At one point, I was doing $20,000 worth of business a month with Brinker alone.

Even when you're buying and selling old horseshoes and milk cans, you can get into trouble with customs. One of our container loads of antiques got stopped at the border. The drug dogs went absolutely nuts. The authorities searched the whole container, looking for drugs. What did they find instead? A cat had crawled into an old stove and had died in there. The dogs had smelled the dead cat and had gone ballistic.

We did so well in the antique business that we cleaned out the area. There was nothing left to buy or sell! Again, we had to look for other ways of making money. We tried to sell into the Mexican market and established an exclusive line of antiques, art, jewelry, saddleblankets, saddles and other leather goods. We got the exclusive rights to distribute Circle-Y saddlery into Mexico. We also hoped to become a distribution center for U.S. goods, but the business never took off.

AFTER THE WEAVING, antiques, metal foundry and a dozen other ideas didn't pan out, we decided to set up a *maquila*, or factory, for making horn furniture. I'd bought horns for years from a trader in Central Texas, Willie Dudly. The owner was about to retire so I said, "I'll buy your horn polishing equipment and we'll start doing it in Mexico."

I had plans for doing horns in a big way—mounted horns, furniture made of horns, a whole variety of home furnishings made of horn. I talked up the project with everyone in Chihuahua and told them that this was going to be the deal that saved our operation. The state government agreed to help us out.

I had the equipment. Now all I needed was the horns. I was buying horns by the crate from an importer in Houston, but I found a much better source for horns in Nigeria, Africa. So I ordered a container of horns shipped from Nigeria to Houston, then trucked to El Paso. We were all set to bring the horns into Chihuahua when we ran into a problem with Mexican federal customs.

Federal Mexican customs asked, "Where are these horns from?" Nigeria. "Nigeria?" Mexico had no trade relations or any other types of relations with Nigeria. So it was impossible for Mexican customs to allow the importation of Nigerian cattle horns into the country.

I was really upset. I called my friends in the Chihuahua state government, "Hey, I need to get these horns down there and customs is giving me problems..."

My buddies said, "OK, we'll try to get it fixed..."

"All right. You better."

A week went by and I called up again. "When are you gonna get me my horns?"

"We're gonna get it cleared pretty soon..."

After a whole month went by, I called up and gave them hell. "Dammit! No wonder Mexico can't do anything! Here you've got somebody waiting with money in hand, jobs for your country, and there's a bunch of government assholes holding up progress. No wonder this is such a backward country." I was redneckin' like a sonofabitch, but I was furious. My whole operation was on hold.

A few days later, my buddy in the Chihuahua state government called me back. "OK. It's done."

What I had failed to realize was how much work my friends in Chihuahua City had done to get me my horns. After my first phone call, they had contacted the Nigerian embassy in Washington and had exchanged agreements. Then Mexico had sent a trade representative to Nigeria, and Nigeria had sent a trade representative to Mexico. The two countries had set up cultural relationships and trade relationships and had produced a manual an inch-and-a-half thick which had been ratified by the Mexican Congress—all in a thirty-day period. I felt like an A-1 prize asshole for carrying on so much. Can you imagine how long a thing like that would have taken in the U.S.? And can you imagine how much it would have cost in terms of lobbyists and political donations? But I was proud of the fact that my little horn factory had brought two nations together.

We polished the horns and made good-looking furniture upholstered with Brazilian cowhides. We even used the horn dust to fertilize the pastures at the ranch. But there was one big problem with the horn business. After we were in operation for about six months, I calculated that I had a three-year supply of horn products. And that was being optimistic. We tried to develop a market within Mexico. But it didn't really work.

Probably in about 1997 we knew it wasn't going to be successful. Business was changing, markets were different. Sometimes you go with your heart rather than your business instincts and this was certainly true in our case. There was no one to blame in this case, not the Mexican Government, not the employees and not ourselves. I can say that we did everything proper, honorably and legal. We paid full social security, insurance and benefits to our employees. Many companies in Mexico do not and sometimes it's hard to compete with others when you play by all the rules. It was not our wishes to close the factories or sell the ranch, but we knew it was what we needed to do since by then we could see there was "no light at the end of the tunnel."

AT THE SAME TIME that we were having troubles in Mexico, our operations in El Paso were hurting as well. 1997 was a bad year for our business. Our income was down about a third of what it had been in 1995. We were unable to make El Cid profitable or break even. Setting up the facility at Rancho El Cid was an amazing adventure but eventually reality set in.

The constant El Cid worries were taking their toll on us, as was the traveling. Normally we drove down to the ranch on Saturday of one week, spent a week at the ranch, then drove back to El Paso and spent a week back up here. Bonnie had back problems and oftentimes had to fly back and forth from the ranch. The constant traveling back and forth was particularly tough on her.

After five years, the ranch was nowhere near self-sufficient. We had tried our best, but as any business person knows there comes a time when you have to cut your losses to survive. It was an exciting project and rewarding. We would not have traded the experience for anything, but we decided that if El Paso Saddleblanket was going to prosper, we had to sell out in Chihuahua and move our operations back north to our weaving factory in Juárez.

We sold Rancho El Cid—or as we fondly called it "The Cash Guzzler"—in 1999 to Mr. Miguel Cerezcerez, a Santa Isabel local who had lived in Los Angeles for the last twenty years. He had done well in the wrought iron business and wanted to come back home to Mexico.

Selling the ranch was not a fast or easy deal. It was hard work. We made a cash sale on the ranch. 1999 turned out to be a very interesting year all around. We had been trimming down for about a year and by mid-1999 we had a skeleton crew of only about eight employees. It had been expensive to pay the severance and other departure costs of the employees. We sold some of the ranch equipment and the horses to our local rancher friends. We sold the foundry equipment, the tractor, vehicles and tools. I gave our donkey herd to the Kachina doll makers in El Chaco when we closed the factory there. We had closed the Chimayo weaving factory in San Andres in 1998 and moved the looms back to El Cid. Next were the 120 or so weaving looms at the ranch. It was sad to see all our hard work and dreams vanishing little by little.

Even though the weaving factory was not successful, mostly due to the high cost of production, I still had the determination and a dream of seeing this part of Chihuahua become a weaving center much like Oaxaca and Jalisco. I knew I had successfully taken a bunch of cowboys in Santa Isabel and transformed some of them into pretty good artists on the loom. We already had some trained weavers, plenty of looms, yarn, and most of all, El Paso Saddleblanket Company was the largest importer and manufacturer of Mexican artesania in the world, which would provide a natural outlet for the production.

I could not bear to see all the work and energy we had put into this project be wasted. There had to be a different way to do it other than in a factory production setting. It would have been smarter to walk off at this point, but I guess I just had something to prove. I became obsessed with planting that little seed that would grow into this HUGE miracle of a success story that would provide hundreds of jobs, introduce sheep again to the area for their wool and on and on. It was not about money at this point. It was a point of pride, maybe stubborn pride on my part. I have to admit, I don't give in to failure easily. Maybe it was ego, maybe it would vindicate the whole weaving factory failure. Other villages in Mexico did it. Things had to start somewhere. There are pottery making villages; wood carving, weaving, leather making, basket making and jewelry making villages. Why couldn't we make our area into a great weaving area?

I called on our friends from the Chihuahua Economic Development Office once again to help us salvage what we could and hopefully establish a weaving center in Chihuahua. I proposed a loose partnership between El Paso Saddleblanket and the Chihuahua state government to open four small weaving co-ops in Santa Isabel and three more in other villages that they could choose. We agreed on the philosophy that the government was there to help the people however possible and not to make a profit. El Paso Saddleblanket would help set up the factories and handle the marketing worldwide. One thing I knew for sure by now was that we were much better at marketing than manufacturing. We agreed that we would donate the looms for Santa Isabel; the state would purchase looms for the other villages and buy our remaining yarn. El Paso Saddleblanket would do all the future purchasing of yarn for a twenty percent fee and also buy all the weaving production from the co-ops that met our quality standards. Each village could locate their factory in a building or have weavers work from their homes, cottage industry style. Our friends in the state government knew us very well by now and quickly agreed to the plan.

We moved the looms and set up the mostly cottage industries with record speed. I bought and shipped a truck load of wool yarn from two carpet mills in Dalton, Georgia. Experienced weavers from Santa Isabel were sent to the three other villages. Two of the villages were very remote. One had only gasoline generators for electrical power. I completed our part of the agreement and turned it over to the state.

Things started going downhill fast. It was an election year so the politicians in Chihuahua City turned things over to the local *presidentes* (mayors). Training money was handed out like candy, products and yarn began to vanish, ghost payrolls appeared and on and on.

Within a few months everything imploded, some of the metal looms were disassembled and used for gates and on doors around the villages. It was horrible. I was devastated and absolutely helpless to do anything except watch everything self destruct. It was very disappointing and I suppose I could have gone into some type of deep depression.

But what the hell! I was now back full-time in El Paso, business was really picking up, I was doing more at the Juárez factory and we had a bunch of new products and samples being made overseas. Things were looking up! 1999 was coming to an end and…

A NEW MILLENNIUM was just around the corner!

OUR COMPANY was doing better than ever financially. And we still kept in close touch with all the friends we made in Chihuahua while we were operating Rancho El Cid.

Even though it was a financial failure from the beginning to the end, I consider Rancho El Cid one of our biggest accomplishments. I have never had as much fun, problems, excitement, worries, adventure, pride and disappointments as I did in those years from 1993 to 1999. Mexico is a beautiful land, but you soon figure out that the customs and the rules are very different. Especially in the countryside, life is gritty and raw. Things we consider normal and routine can not be taken for granted. It is not a place for a weak stomach and in time it will harden you. There is a fine art to living and working there. There is a tough macho mentality yet compassion and honor rules. One must be careful not to let people mistake your kindness for weakness. Land owners (the employers) are expected to maintain certain traditions and responsibilities. The worker mentality tends to be more socialistic. Domestic abuse, alcoholism and animal abuse are common. Many Mexicans do not have the means to feed their families.

Life is hard for many people and yet we had to accept the fact that we could not be all things to all people. We learned their ways and were accepted and respected in the community because we were always honest, hardworking people and respected people's families and their culture. It is impossible for me to describe all my feelings about Santa Isabel, Chihuahua, Mexico.

I felt a deep relief when we left Santa Isabel. But at the same time I felt a true pride of accomplishment for what we did in those six years at El Cid. To this day I still dream of El Cid at night and reflect back everyday on our friends and the crazy things we did down there. It's been many years now, but somehow a part of Bonnie and I will always be in Santa Isabel. We still keep in touch and go back from time to time. It's beautiful.

Chapter Nineteen

The Wholesale Experience

*"January 1, 2000...El Paso Saddleblanket
Company closed it's doors to the public.
Wholesale only to stores and dealers..."*

 IT WAS ABOUT MID-MAY 1999 by the time we were completely out of El Cid. Sold, moved, and out! The '90s had been good, particularly the early '90s. Those were recession years in America, but El Paso Saddleblanket has always done very well in recessions. We sold to a lot of folks who were unemployed or needed extra income. It's one thing to sell to the "hobby" or "fun" vendors who enjoy selling our products at craft shows, fairs, home shows, and such but who do not have to sell. The "hobby" vendor is totally different from the unemployed person who MUST SELL in order to make ends meet and feed the family. In tough economic times, a lot of hard-selling customers came to us, and almost all of them did well, since we offered them good products at affordable prices. Ambitious vendors who worked hard were almost always successful.

The mid-'90s were good steady business years and then things started slowly slipping in '96; 1997 was still profitable but down from earlier years primarily because we were occupied with working and having fun at the ranch.

When we made the decision to close the El Cid factory in 1998 we started concentrating more on the wholesale side of the business in El Paso and developing new textile products from overseas. As we were closing down the Mexico operation in 1998 we were going through a lot of changes in El Paso. Three of the five major hotels downtown closed, including the two hundred room International Hotel next to the store. Freeway construction, poor management of our Convention Bureau, the drug wars and murders in Juárez and a few other things caused a slow-down in tourism.

Our retail business declined but our wholesale business was having HUGE growth. By early 1999 we had two additional large warehouses. The central office and shipping department doubled in size. Our merchandise strategy also changed. We had been a real tourist attraction, a colorful Mexican mercado with great souvenirs and trinkets.

This was great fun and we made a nice mark-up. But it was difficult to make money: you prepay the vendors in Mexico, go through all the hassles of Customs in both Mexico and the U.S., pay freight and duty, transport goods first to the warehouse and then to the store, unpack, mark prices, sell, make tickets, repack, box the product for the customers…and on and on.

We slowly replaced much of the trinkets and souvenirs with higher grade products. We lost a lot of sales because many of our customers were either poorer people from El Paso and Mexico or low-budget tourist travelers. Retail traffic was down but our wholesale walk-in traffic was up. Most of our wholesale customers were not interested in souvenir curios anyway. And the wholesale orders from our catalogs were setting sales records every month. We started experimenting with a new concept of advertising and selling called the internet. We missed Rancho El Cid, but an exciting new transformation was taking place in El Paso.

• • •

I BELIEVE in listening to your business because I know it will talk to you.

By this time, my business was telling me to close the retail operation and concentrate exclusively on wholesale. A wholesale operation is more efficient. Fewer employees. No marking or displaying. No shoplifting problems. Less chance of injuries and lawsuits. No retail advertising cost. Higher numbers in sales transactions. Better space utilization. And we could close Saturdays, thus having happier employees. Our wholesale profits were lower, but we made up for the lower margins with higher volume and lower overhead. Bonnie and I had been working nonstop for twenty-five years and knew nothing else. Our business was our life and neither of us had hobbies or social obligations. We never took pleasure vacations or cruises; all of our travels had always been for business in one way or another. We thought that being tourists laying around the beach somewhere was both boring and nonproductive. Bonnie and I were in our fifties by then and started talking about taking time off—whatever that was.

Although we had planned it a few months earlier, we made the announcement around the middle of November, in time for the Christmas season. We liquidated most of the souvenir curios and Indian jewelry at discounted prices. There was a lot of negative press about us closing a downtown institution after being open to the public in that location for thirteen years. We had lots of calls from unhappy longtime customers.

I think one of the reasons for the complaints was the fact that local El Paso and Las Cruces people could get out of taking visitors to Juárez by taking them to El Paso Saddleblanket Company and explaining to them that we had more items than the markets in Juárez and at a better price. This was true, plus Juárez had problems with long lines, aggressive street hustlers and rip-off prices. The once thriving shopping strip on Juárez Avenue had now mostly turned into underage drinking places and stores that catered to the locals: shoe stores, wedding dress stores and lots of pharmacies. While some customers whined, our overall business was very good.

The situation surrounding us in downtown El Paso was not so good. In fact, downtown was sliding into ruin. More vacant buildings. More street people begging. Dirtier streets and sidewalks.

But the more things went down around us, the more our business went up. Through time, our store had gotten further away from the cute Mexican market look and had gone to a more gritty warehouse look with merchandise stacked to the ceiling. We were less of an attraction for the retail buying tourist, but the wholesale buyers seemed more impressed than ever. As the wholesale side of our business continued to zoom up, we made the decision...

"JANUARY 1, 2000...EL PASO SADDLEBLANKET COM-PANY CLOSED IT'S DOORS TO THE PUBLIC. WHOLESALE ONLY TO STORES AND DEALERS..."

We did it!

Chapter Twenty

Hillsboro

"I think we were ready for
some new project or adventure."

AFTER WE SOLD EL CID in 1999, we really missed having property in a rural area—the open spaces, room for the dogs (four German shepherds by this time) and just a place to go to. Business was good and we had made some money on the actual sale of the El Cid property (not the overall business venture), so we decided in 2001 that we wanted to buy a large ranch within easy driving distance of El Paso.

The search began. We looked at property in West Texas and all over southern New Mexico. All kinds of places. Some of the ranches were too far away, some were too desolate. Many were very overpriced. A lot of the ranches were twenty to sixty thousand acres: too big, too much of a cattle operation and too much work. The choices seemed either one or two-acre "ranchettes" or the big spreads. We would have liked to have had two to five sections. Also in New Mexico most of the larger ranches were a combination of deeded, Bureau of Land Management land and state lease land, which meant a lot of government control which I wanted no part of. We looked around for about six months without much luck.

One Friday night I called Bob Shufelt, an artist friend of ours, who had a home and art gallery in Hillsboro, New Mexico. Bob "Shoofly" Shufelt is probably the best-known Western pencil artist in America today. He told me that he had just bought a ranch in Lake Valley, about fifteen miles outside of Hillsboro. Bob and his wife Julie were going to sell their beautiful historic adobe home in Hillsboro. So Bonnie and I agreed to drive up the next morning and take a look.

Hillsboro, New Mexico is an historic, high-desert mining town that was thriving from the late 1880s to about 1930. The town once had a population of around three thousand with some fourteen saloons and many brothels. Today Hillsboro is a village of about 250 residents; many of them are artists and writers.

I like to call it a poor man's Santa Fe. It has two nice restaurants, two bed and breakfast inns, several galleries, antique shops and the famous S Bar X Saloon where artist and ranch cowboys mingle peacefully (most of the time). There is a clock maker, weaver, potter, furniture maker, several photographers, many painters and even a Hollywood film maker (not to mention several bullshit artists). There are some historic buildings, an Old-West-style boardwalk street front and an interesting cemetery. Percha Creek goes through the middle of town. Nine miles west of Hillsboro is another famous old ghost town: Kingston, which is one thousand feet higher in elevation and has a pine tree alpine climate with the Gila Forest surrounding it. The whole area is beautiful and virtually undiscovered. Hillsboro—these days known for its labor day Apple Festival—is only two hours north of El Paso but neither Bonnie or I had ever been there.

WE DROVE OUT to Shoofly's Flying J Ranch and had some of Julie's famous cowboy biscuits and gravy. We saw his studio and their stables with fine horses. We looked over his western memorabilia collection and saw Julie's collection of just about everything: antiques, Mexican artesania, art, pottery, Indian artifacts. You name it, Julie collected it. We went into town and looked at their beautiful adobe, but quickly realized there was not enough yard for four rowdy German shepherd dogs.

On the way out of town we saw a beautiful fenced one-acre lot with a kinda hillbilly old house and a detached garage. The house wasn't much but we saw some possibilities. There was also about thirty acres joining that property that had Percha Creek going through the middle of it. That lot had huge forty-foot cottonwood trees, pine trees, cactus and lots of grass along with beautiful river rocks. The land was open and accessible.

The house was only about two blocks from the Old-West-style street front, post office, volunteer fire department, community center and library. Both properties were priced right and we quickly made the deals. Later we found out the thirty-acre property was actually Old Hillsboro before a fire destroyed it and the creek changed course around the turn of the century. The property had a wild orchard and was inhabited by deer, javelina hogs, fox, bear, bob cats, mountain lions, quail and lots of white wing dove. Absolutely pristine.

Bonnie did a great job remodeling the place. She completely redid the main house, added a separate luxury apartment suite and turned the detached double garage into a funky guest house. She did it in the modern Southwest, Taos style with large covered porches, new tin roofs and decorative tile murals inside and out. We installed new landscaping and a beautiful wrought iron fence around the main compound. It looked like a golf course. The thirty acres behind the compound were left natural. We put out feeders and watched a parade of wildlife everyday.

It was our getaway and we enjoyed doing the project as well as spending most weekends in Hillsboro. I quickly made friends with a lot of the townsfolk, including Rick Tafoya, a part Mescalaro Indian who was born and raised in Hillsboro. We spent a lot of time fishing in the Rio Grande River and several large lakes nearby. Bonnie and some of the other animal lovers in Hillsboro had a booth at the Annual Apple Festival to sell products donated by El Paso Saddleblanket to raise funds for a local effort to neuter all the feral cats in town. The $2,700 they raised took care of that problem. We also teamed up with local rancher Pat Jones and his wife Nancee to sponsor the monthly team ropings at the Way Out West

Rodeo Arena on their ranch. We entertained a lot of friends, spent lots of time with the dogs and enjoyed this stage of our life.

By 2004 the business was in great shape and I think we were ready for some new project or adventure. I had turned sixty by then, and although I wanted new challenges, I didn't want to get too wild or crazy and take a chance on any business setbacks at this point. I kept a close eye on the internet and began to understand it. I believed that it had endless possibilities. This proved to be true.

ONE OF THE MOST FUN and rewarding things during this time was the college class I taught.

Imagine that. Me, a C student and sophomore college flunk-out, teaching a class for college accredited hours to the six top senior business scholars at the University of Texas at El Paso (UTEP). Dr. Frank Hoy, dean of the School of Business, handpicked the students. He is a leading recognized authority on franchising.

We got to know Dr. Hoy in the early '90s when he would bring visitors from all over the world to visit El Paso Saddleblanket. He also purchased gift items to carry to his friends on his foreign travels. In 1991 Bonnie and I hosted a reception at our Pennsylvania Circle home for Dr. Hoy, his staff and a touring group of about twenty Russians studying American-style capitalism. They must have liked what they saw in this country because we heard later that about half of them defected.

Throughout the years we have had a lot of people ask us about opening some type of El Paso Saddleblanket franchise store. From time to time we have had people open a store featuring mostly products from our company. Some have done pretty well, including one very successful company in Australia who started small and later was buying container loads. I have always advocated for stores and dealers to stock large supplies of our products, but never particularly like the idea of telling a franchisee what he could or could not do or sell. Same thing about giving out "Exclusive Distributorships for Areas." I always remembered what Mauricio and Julio Sidransky—the Polish-Mexican-Jewish traders from Juárez—used to say about "exclusive" deals back in the '70s. They had a Yiddish saying that "There is one God, but not one customer."

I had often asked Dr. Hoy's business advice on various subjects; we had even discussed franchising some Saddleblanket stores on several occasions. I had thought about it, but somehow never could put together any significant concept.

He suggested that I teach a class at UTEP. Not only would the students learn first hand about the import business from me, but I could learn about franchising and about some modern business techniques from them.

It was settled. Class was to begin in the spring semester, January 2005.

Dr. Hoy taught an honors class Mondays and Wednesdays. I would lead a two-hour class and two-hour workshop on Fridays at El Paso Saddleblanket Company. The class had two girls, four boys, all of them Hispanic, with three from Mexico and three Americans. Just like Donald Trump in *The Apprentice* I explained our mission was to set up and organize our new theme stores that would be called El Paso Saddleblanket DIRECT.

I must say that these were some of the finest young people I have ever met or had the pleasure to work with. We worked to create prototype stores, market analyses, feasibility studies and franchise concepts. I never imagined how much work and time all this would be. Or how interesting and fun it would be to be around the excitement, energy and brainpower of these kids. We studied every aspect of the franchises in detail and published a complete summary. I spent a lot of time just hanging out with the students. The class finished up in May; all of them made an A+. When Dr. Hoy thanked us I confessed to him that it was one of the most rewarding things I had ever participated in and admitted that the whole thing was way out of character for me.

• • •

THE PERIOD from 2000 through 2005 was the golden years for us. Business was increasing. As our expenses for advertising, fixtures, equipment and overhead decreased, we had real financial strength for the first time— we were debt free. The whole operation was almost on automatic pilot.

We were closed on weekends, which gave us more time to relax. Bonnie played her grand piano more, we traveled some and I finished the original edition of *Rugs to Riches*.

Life was pretty good. But then life has a way of surprising you.

BOTH OF MY PARENTS passed away during this time. This gave me, my sister and my nephews and niece the responsibility of settling the estate and running Fun Valley, my parent's resort in Colorado. My sister Melba is very solid, sensible and fair. It was decided long ago that she would be the one to lead and carry on with the Henson family businesses. This was a very smart move on my father's part and things have been running smooth with her in charge. Frankly, I loved growing up at Fun Valley and learning the restaurant and hospitality business, but it was never my ambition to be in that business.

I was especially happy with our achievements and had very little to be worried about. On the other hand, things were going so well, I actually began feeling a little bored and unchallenged.

Bonnie and I have always been conservative in business. First of all I never had the stomach for much risk taking. I never admired the crap-shooting, bet-the-whole-farm-type of reckless deal junkies. Some make it big, but most eventually go under.

Do you ever remember seeing the macho cowboy T-shirts with the slogan "No Fear"? Well, I always wanted to have one printed for me that says "Total Fear," at least when it comes to business. I never wanted to lose any ground or have setbacks.

Usually when you read biographies of great business people, most have had some huge disaster of some type: big fire, natural disaster, bankruptcies and so on. In that sense we have been very lucky. The whole El Cid episode was a money loser, 9-11 slowed things a few months, some products were not as popular as we planned. In the late '80s pastel color and jewel-tone rugs went out of style, causing us to sell some at a slight loss. But other than that we have not had much drama or disasters.

I still consider the Old West Hotel a great achievement, mainly because that's were I met Bonnie.

To me, May of 2005 was the end of what I will always call those golden years. That same month something BIG was about to happen.

Chapter Twenty-one

The New El Paso Saddleblanket World Headquarters

"Early to bed, early to rise, work like hell,
and AD-VER-TISE."

—TED TURNER

 IN LATE 2004 and early 2005 we were looking at several expansion possibilities. We had some blue prints drawn up for a huge new "Highway Store" Trading Post we wanted to build west of El Paso on Interstate 10. Tanny Berg—a long time friend and very successful real estate developer (among many other things)—was building his second Microtel motel franchise on a large parcel of land he owned. We planned a joint venture partnership deal on a building to be built next door. El Paso Saddleblanket would do a long-term lease with an option to purchase everything at a later date. We designed this huge forty-thousand-square-foot trading post to look like an Aztec village. It featured an eighty-foot observation tower with a viewing platform at the top that would enable people to see three states and two countries. Tanny was a big thinker, had the resources to do it and was excited about the challenge of the project.

We all loved the idea, wrestled with the concept and crunched the numbers. It's always very tempting to get caught up in emotion and excitement, especially a never-been-done project like this. There was no guarantee this mega-monster was going to be successful.

We began to study the "what if" scenarios and tried to figure exit strategies. Even though I had invested a lot of time and money in the plan, we decided in the end that it was a risk that we were unwilling to take. We will never know for sure, but as I look back now, I am inclined to believe it would have been a success. Big time.

By April we were on another deal to open a smaller trading post in Old Mesilla outside of Las Cruces, New Mexico, which is about forty miles northwest of El Paso. This was to be our prototype and first of the planned franchises that would be called El Paso Saddleblanket DIRECT.

We had picked a one-and-a-half-acre site on Interstate 10 that seemed to have everything we wanted. It was near a freeway exit, sitting in between a newly opened Appleby's Restaurant and a 150-room motel. There were four other hotels within walking distance and two nice RV parks. The six students, Bonnie and I had decided on a more practical eight to ten-thousand-square-foot trading post, which would leave us enough room for a convenience store with gas pumps at the back of the property. Two other friends, Meier Marcus and Bob Ayub, had the land and we were working with them to either buy or form another joint venture similar to what Tanny and us were planning earlier on with the big trading post. The students were excited and very supportive. We were close to making the deal and opening our first of several planned stores. We had planned to open each store and then sell to operators who would become wholesale customers for El Paso Saddleblanket products. We calculated that each store could realistically do up to a million dollars per year.

On May 13, 2005 I received a call from real estate agent Paul Connington telling me of his new listing, just on the market: the Freeway Bowling Lanes. The property was four acres on a freeway frontage with a one-acre bowling center. The building had a wide runway down the center and eighteen lanes on each side of the runway. There was a large billiard parlor near the front and a complete coffee shop and a separate cocktail lounge in the back part. There were offices, storage rooms, maintenance workshops and a fairly large conference room in the back. There were three acres of parking for cars, trucks and RVs. Traditionally bowling centers have very good roofs and air conditioning systems, which was also a big plus. Freeway Bowling Lanes was across the freeway from the largest and busiest shopping mall in town and was on Interstate 10 in almost the exact center of El Paso. The traffic count was officially 199,000 cars per day. We toured the facility and quickly decided to scrap the plans for the El Paso Saddleblanket DIRECT prototype store and attempt to buy the future home of what would become The El Paso Saddleblanket World Headquarters.

We knew from day one that this was not going to be easy, but were determined to make this deal by almost any means possible. Apart from needing several million dollars, there was already an offer on the table and another buyer hot on the trail. This in just the first two days it was on the market. We immediately went to Bank of the West and to our surprise after only about a fifteen minute discussion with Jon Rogers, Larry Pattan and Rick Francis we received an unofficial "nod." In 1991 we had invested in and became stockholders in this new bank. Bank of the West now has seven banks in El Paso with more planned.

The property owner was from out of town and could not be reached because he was on a cruise in the Caribbean. It took a little detective work, but we managed to fax him an offer direct to the cruise liner. The next day we received word that he had accepted our offer.

We had the closing set for June 13th and had managed to keep things very hush-hush for the most part. Only a few people knew about the deal, but somehow the press still heard something was up. Luckily we managed to dodge them until a couple of days before the closing. Then the bomb dropped. The previous owner only gave his employees a few days notice before the pink slips went out; everyone was upset. Also the bowling leagues, the customers, the various suppliers and just about everyone else was in an uproar. The owner quickly left town after closing, and we were left holding a time bomb.

The Freeway Bowling Lanes was built in 1957 and was an El Paso landmark. The bar was a famous watering hole with a large local following including generations of people with volumes of memories. The restaurant was known for the best green enchiladas in El Paso.

This was big news in El Paso and I was stunned that most of the publicity was negative. Closing of a tradition, the end of an era, a sad day in sports history and so on. One television station even did a teary interview with an old couple who had gotten married there in 1958 and showed photographs of the then young and happy newlyweds. The Black Baptist Bowling League and many others were pissed off. Some people had shoes and bowling balls locked in the lockers.

The truth was that the Freeway Bowling Lanes was neglected, run down and outdated: its wooden lanes were no longer popular, the equipment in need of repair, and it was losing money. It was for sale and all we did was buy it. Unfortunately the media and a lot of others did not have a clue that one of the biggest attractions in West Texas was about to be born.

After our offer was accepted in May 2005, we had plenty of decisions to make and lots of work ahead of us. With the exception of the pool tables we bought a running turnkey operation complete, including all the bowling equipment, restaurant, bar and on and on. Bowling shoes, the food in the refrigerators, tools, tables and chairs, bowling ball polisher, and thirty-six lanes—each containing sixty feet of maple hardwood flooring and an A-2 Brunswick pinsetter—were all ours.

I remembered watching "Bonanza" on television as a kid. After surveying our latest purchase my first thought was "What do we do now, Pa?"

WE ORIGINALLY calculated that the transformation would not be completed and opened until early 2006. The first order of business was to close the restaurant and bar and sell off the bowling equipment. We gave the food to our employees and sent a truckload of restaurant appliances, coolers, utensils, booths, tables and bowling trophies to Fun Valley. I put the bowling equipment on E-bay and almost immediately started getting inquiries.

I learned a lot about the bowling center business real fast. Modern facilities no longer use the hardwood lanes, but rather some acrylic material that is better and easier to maintain. The Brunswick A-2 pinsetters have long been replaced by new more efficient technology as well as modern scorekeeping screens. Besides that, there were warehouses around the country full of this outdated equipment. Some things are sold for parts and certain model pinsetters are sold to third world countries. Most of the inquiries were interested in shoes, parts and other selected items.

I realized we had a big problem. How do we sell this? If we scrapped everything, there would be a huge cost in labor, not to mention we didn't have a clue where we would dump it. We were also in a time crunch and could not start the moving and remodeling until we cleared the place out. In the mean time I ran some classified ads and sold some miscellaneous odd-lot junk, supplies and other things to salvage dealers from Juárez.

I was really starting to get concerned. Things were basically on hold. We had to do something.

I was never much of a believer in miracles but I must say this is about as close as I've ever seen. I have a pretty strong Texas drawl, but one day I got a call from Selma, Alabama, from a guy with such a heavy southern accent that by comparison it made me sound like some college English professor. As it turned out, these four young partners had a successful small twelve-lane bowling center and had a clientele of mostly poor African-American folks. At first they wanted only twelve lanes and twelve pinsetters for a possible new location in a nearby small town. We talked back and forth over a few days and I e-mailed them some photo images. They were my kind of people: simple and direct. I convinced them they could buy all thirty six lanes and open either two or possibly three smaller centers. I had been asking one thousand dollars per lane. Finally I said, "Bring me $12,000 cash and I'll give you every damn thing in this place that has anything to do with bowling on two conditions: I want this place totally stripped clean and I want you out and gone in ten days."

We made the verbal agreement on a Friday in the first week of July.

Then Bonnie and I took the dogs and went to Hillsboro for the weekend. On Monday morning about 9 A.M. I received a call from them. They had seven guys in a caravan of three pick-up trucks and they had been driving eighteen hours nonstop from Alabama. They were in Van Horn, Texas, about two hours out of El Paso. I gave them directions to Freeway Lanes and suggested they grab a motel room, rest up, and we have some barbecue over at my house later. After that we could further discuss this giant upcoming moving project. "Mr. Henson, we appreciate your sure-nuff kind invitation, but if it's all the same to you, we would like to start workin' right away, so if you can just meet us there, that would be mighty good," said Andy.

We went to meet the Alabama boys not knowing exactly what to expect, but I guess to describe this crew as "colorful" would be the understatement of the day. Maybe if central casting were looking for some ragtag Confederate soldiers for a sequel to *Gone with the Wind* they would consider this a jackpot.

After a brief tour, the guys backed up their pick-ups and unloaded a large assortment of tools and pallet jacks. They brought sleeping bags; their plan was to work around the clock and grab a little sleep from time to time, which was great as far as we were concerned. I helped arrange twelve to fifteen temporary labor guys from RMT Staffing and some fifty-three-foot tractor trailers to be loaded with equipment and hauled to Alabama as each trailer was filled. We wound up sending a total of seven trailers, each very full. I have never witnessed anything like this. It was about 105 degrees outside and as grueling a work as imaginable. They worked nonstop and never left the building except to get fried chicken and Chinese takeout. The last trailer was loaded and took off for Alabama about 4 P.M. Friday. They got motel rooms, cleaned up and came back to Freeway Lanes where El Paso Saddleblanket threw a big barbecue, with plenty of beer and Jack Daniels, for the Alabama boys, some of the temps and our own crew.

They left the next morning having never seen any other part of El Paso.

• • •

AFTER the Alabama boys left, things started to go a little faster. Inside the building, there was a big sunken trench about eight-foot wide and a foot deep on both sides that needed to be filled. This is where the pinsetters had been installed. After much debate we decided the fastest thing to do would be to knock some holes in the side of the building, run a large hose and pump the cement from the trucks. We removed most of the restaurant and bar equipment pretty fast.

One day as we were removing one of the stoves we punctured a gas line in the wall. Gas started spraying everywhere. So like the little Dutch boy holding the water leak in the dam, Cosme—one of our employees— goes over and sticks his finger in the hole. He kept the gas from escaping while the rest of us were running around trying to figure out how to cut the gas off.

I bought an old twenty-seven-foot U-Haul truck, sight unseen, over the telephone from someone in Albuquerque and we began the move. We purchased about a dozen forty-foot metal containers, placed them in the back parking lot and quickly moved all the products from Warehouse #2. (Warehouse #1 is in Juárez. At the same time we renewed the lease on the ten-thousand-square-foot Warehouse #3 in El Paso for another year. It was about a mile from the old downtown store.) We had a big moving sale at the downtown store, knowing that the more we sold the less we had to move. Remember, we had been closed to the public for about five years at that point. We had a respectable turnout for the sale even though I had expected more.

We had a large work force and things really began to move. Originally the plan was to open in January 2006 but we saw an opportunity to open sooner. Eighty truckloads later, the old downtown store was empty.

In June I had made a deal with a large tannery owner from Brazil to come in as partner on our old downtown location. He helped his son start a furniture factory in Novo Hamburgo, Brazil that would make chairs, sofas and other products upholstered with "hair on" cowhides from his tannery. The plan was to have the wholesale showroom outlet here in

El Paso and then we would ship all over the U.S. and into Canada. He changed his mind later, which I believe was because he feared too much competition would come from China. He is a very smart man and it was probably a good decision.

Anyway, there was plenty of work to do opening the new World Headquarters of El Paso Saddleblanket. I'm actually glad we didn't do it because I didn't need the distraction.

WE HIRED my second cousin, Luc Wells, as the new general manager shortly before we opened. Luc was a graduate of the Naval Academy in Annapolis where he had played football and studied Spanish. He then went on active duty in Iraq. When he returned he was a Marine Captain and a decorated war hero. After four years at the Academy and five years as a Marine, we thought he was exactly what El Paso Saddleblanket needed. His experience in leadership, work discipline, computers—plus his ability to speak Spanish—turned out to be a good move.

THE DOORS to the new one-acre World Headquarters opened on October 1st, 2005 with an inexperienced new crew, half-opened boxes and unfinished shelving. It was less than spectacular, but we managed to start doing business.

Looking back now I know I made at least two big mistakes (probably more).

First was the lack of initial advertising for the retail side of our business. The wholesale part was solid and steady, but we had been out of the retail business for almost five years and many people still believed we were not open to the public. Since I had spent a lot of money on the move, I thought I could save some money by not advertising as much. Instead I tried to get the word out by press releases, free publicity and word of mouth. I did buy about thirty large highway billboards on both sides of El Paso and some minimal newspaper and radio ads. I even ran a few TV spots.

If I had it to do over, I would have spent much more on advertising the opening. Ted Turner—founder of CNN and an advertising genius—used to say: "Early to bed, early to rise, work like hell, and AD-VER-TISE."
I believe him!

I THINK THE SECOND MISTAKE we made was the entire concept of the World Headquarters. Before we closed the old downtown store to the public in 2000 it was a fun shopping experience with a Mexican mercado atmosphere. We sold a lot of trinket curio items as well as a lot of middle and higher range products.

Now we had decided we wanted to create a new identity as an outlet type place with big stacks of selected limited merchandise with simple signs and very basic, drab decor. The big stacks had prices like $28 each; if a customer bought three it would be $25 each; six would cost $23 each; and so on. Then we ran a partition down the middle of the store. This left half the store for a warehouse area for wholesale buyers and the other half would be for the walk-in (retail buyers) trade. We had hoped it would give the retail buyer the feeling they were buying direct from a manufac-turer (which they were) rather than some Route 66 type roadside tourist trap. We placed a desk staffed with our sales people at the front door in hopes of interviewing and qualifying buyers. We knew for sure that we did not care to be in the postcard, rubber tomahawk, cheap Mexican pottery, trinket type business again.

When El Paso Saddleblanket World Headquarters opened on October 1, 2005 the wholesale side was still very good. But the retail part was only a mild success. Although we were selling products, I noticed that the retail side was not living up to what I thought was its full potential. First off, the staffed desk in the front was an obstacle people really didn't like. So was the partition down the middle. The concept of big stacks with quantity prices did not go over well because most people only wanted one of an item but felt ripped off because we were offering the quantity retail buyers a cheaper price.

Our warehouse concept was drab and boring. Many of the customers who used to shop with us were whining about not having the selection we used to, and so on.

Generally speaking, wholesalers do not make the transition into retail business very well. Some wholesalers think they are too smart and many others are used to talking with business owners and have little patience with retail consumers. Just the opposite, people with a retail background usually can do very well in the wholesale business. Some places are decorated too cute or too snobby, giving the customer the feeling everything is expensive and overpriced. Some places are over decorated and become some museum that people enjoy but wind up not buying from. But on the other hand a nice store should not look like a junk store or a low-end flea market. Lots of thought needs to be put into these things before you open a new store. I have personally always liked the Ford-and-Chevrolet, middle-of-the-road type business because more of the population fits in this category.

Things were just not working out like we had hoped on the retail side. We even considered closing the retail part and going back to wholesale only, but with a four-acre freeway location like this it would be a shame. Some redesigning, rethinking and rearranging needed to be done. We needed to reinvent the retail side of our business, because even though we were doing business, we were off the mark. Things needed to change.

Chapter Twenty-two

Trading Post Events

"Events draw people and help your business."

ABOUT FOUR TO SIX MONTHS after we opened we started making major changes. Our initial theme was a plain warehouse outlet with minimal selection of goods and mountains of products stacked high. Our new concept would be a colorful trading-post atmosphere with Spanish guitar music, great displays and more variation of merchandise.

Once we decided on that direction, changes came very fast. We removed the partition down the middle and the registration desk at the front door. The Oriental & Persian rug inventory doubled. We put in ten showcases full of turquoise and silver jewelry. Those cases were so successful that we kept adding more until we finally had over fifty showcases of jewelry. We moved the three-thousand-square-foot central office from the front of the building to the back and filled the front space with beautiful pottery, pewter, artifacts and antiques from Mexico. We added new products like mounted horns, cow and buffalo skulls, more styles of baskets, rattlesnake products, a new line of high-end saddles and a tack department, more leather goods of all kinds, glassware and more home decor. I dramatically increased the TV, radio, newspaper and magazine advertising. And of course, we bought more billboards (we're up to about fifty). This was a big expense, but slowly it began to pay off. In a matter of a few short months we transformed the World Headquarters into a "one-acre shopping ADVENTURE."

Another thing that worked well for us was various events and promotions. One of the first events we tried was a Winter Open House that we invited everyone we could think of to. Plus we did some major advertising. There was live music, food, refreshments, some special arts and crafts demonstrations and more.

The event was a mild success. Our theory was to just get as much traffic in as possible and hope that word would spread about the new look of El Paso Saddleblanket Company.

The next notable event was what we called the Media Appreciation Fiesta. We invited everyone in the El Paso print, TV and radio media for a big barbecue and awards presentation. We had a live weather broadcast from the store. Cara Wells (Luc's wife) made the presentations and Bill Blazeik of The Convention and Visitors Bureau was the emcee. We gave out ten awards; the media folks loved it and really enjoyed socializing with each other. We had about three hundred people turn out. The event was a huge success so we decided we definitely needed more big events.

The biggest event we have ever had—probably the biggest event we will ever have—was the Don Haskins book signing in June of 2006.

In 1966 Coach Don Haskins of Texas Western College (now the University of Texas El Paso) had won the prestigious NCAA Basketball Tournament with a starting line up of five African-American players. Haskins coached at UTEP for the next thirty-eight years despite many good offers to coach elsewhere. He had a phenomenal winning record and is one of the most revered and popular personalities in the entire Southwest.

A book by Haskins and nationally known sportswriter Dan Wetzel called *Glory Road* was later made into a movie starring Josh Lucas. The movie won an ESPY award in 2006, which in sports movies is the same as an Oscar at the Academy Awards.

Coach Haskins is a very modest person who has helped many people go on to greater things. For years he would collect and gather food to distribute to needy people in Mexico and El Paso. I didn't follow sports much and never met Coach Haskins until one particularly cold day when he came to me wanting to buy blankets to distribute along with his food baskets. Over his objection, I ended up donating some blankets to the cause. He was grateful and we became good friends. He came to Hillsboro a lot.

We decided to do a book signing with Coach Haskins at El Paso Saddleblanket in June of 2006. He had already had several successful signings at Barnes & Noble and at the UTEP book store in January so he didn't think he would have much of a turnout for another book signing. But then the movie won the ESPY award and the studio released the movie on DVD in May. The coach had his own clothing line and speaking engagements around the country. Coach Haskins and the 1966 team were even invited to the White House for a special screening with President Bush and the First Lady. There was a lot of hype nationwide at the time.

I wanted to do this book signing and get maximum exposure. So we decided that we would sell the newly released *Glory Road* DVD as well as the book for Haskins to sign. He would also autograph sports memorabilia, clothing articles, posters, basketballs and anything else for a $5 fee to be donated to charity.

Remembering the recent success of our Media Appreciation Awards, I invited all the media to a press release party & barbecue to announce the upcoming book signing on the following Saturday. All four major TV network stations showed up, as well as two from Juárez and a host of radio stations and print press, including the local gay newspaper. We had the announcement on every sports news broadcast in town that Wednesday night.

AT 8:30 A.M. on Saturday June 10, 2006—the day of the scheduled 11 A.M. book signing—I got a call from my general manager Luc Wells. He called from his cell phone on the way to open up saying there were about twenty cars already in our parking lot. Something told me that this was not going to be an ordinary day.

By the time Coach Haskins and co-author Dan Wetzel arrived, there were fifteen hundred people in the store, our three-acre parking lot was full and no parking places could be found within a block of the El Paso Saddleblanket World Headquarters. The press showed up in full force. The line to buy books and numbered autograph tickets snaked all around the inside of the store. Bonnie and I served cold water to the hundreds of people in line but we knew that there was no way we could finish by 4 P.M. Jeff Limberg, a friend and local sports personality, went around and announced that we would have to continue the book signing the next Saturday because we had sold six hundred more autograph tickets that the Coach could sign. On the 6 and 10 P.M. news that night every TV station showed the huge lines at Saddleblanket with short clips of Haskins signing books. The leading sports story in the *El Paso Times* and the *Las Cruces Sun-News* that Sunday was about the phenomenal book signing.

The next Saturday was almost as busy but we were better prepared. Again, we oversold the books, DVDs and autograph tickets by about three hundred this time. Again, Jeff went around and made the announcement that we would be going into double overtime for the third Saturday in a row. Again, great 6 and 10 P.M. TV news coverage and leading newspaper sports stories on Sunday.

The last Saturday was busy, but without the craziness of the first two. Hey, we were getting to be old hands at this now.

Coach signed steadily all day and we wound up finishing the last autograph at 4:30. We broke out the tequila while Coach sent Beto Fournier, his assistant (and crony), out to his pick-up to get his coyote and duck callers. Then the legendary seventy-six-year-old coach proceeded to demonstrate the fine art of duck calling for the next three hours.

At this time, I was starting to think to myself, "There could be some future opportunities to this book signing business."

• • •

I HAD MET Kinky Friedman a few months earlier, at about the time he announced he was going to run for governor of Texas. Kinky is an iconic Texas musician and multi-book writer. He was part of the 1970s outlaw country music movement here in Texas when he, Willie Nelson, Waylon Jennings and others merged the hippies and cowboys into a sort of Texas-style country-western/rock and roll sound.

A few months after we met his El Paso campaign manager notified me about Kinky's planned fundraiser at the Camino Real Hotel on Sunday. Remembering the recent success of the Haskins event, I suggested a book signing at the World Headquarters the Monday after the fundraiser. It was short notice and on a Monday besides, but we were confident we could have a good turn out. The TV reporters showed up, Kinky lit up a cigar inside the store live on a Channel 7 interview and the phones went wacko. The fundraiser at the Camino Real Hotel drew thirty-five people; the Kinky Friedman book signing at El Paso Saddleblanket World Headquarters drew over four hundred. We were happy, and he was very, very happy.

I'll never forget what his departing words to me were: "Dusty, when I get to be governor...you're on Easy Street." And with that, my last words to him were, "Kinky, you just got my vote!" He came in a distant fourth place in the Texas governor's race, but my guess is that his book sales and music business went up. (I know for sure, the saddleblanket business went up.)

"Hmmm...I think I like book signings..."

IN JULY, we teamed up with Adair Margo, a very successful local gallery owner, to plan the Great Southwest Book Fair and Sale which we held at El Paso Saddleblanket World Headquarters on September 16, 2006. Adair is well connected and she also happens to be one of First Lady Laura Bush's closest friends, and the Chairman of the President's Council on the Arts and the Humanities. Thanks to Adair and husband Dee Margo—Texas state senator candidate at the time—we got an official proclamation from the President and First Lady.

We managed to bring Senator Peggy Rosson out of retirement to help, as well as young socialite Asia Zaragoza. Channel 9 KTSM-TV, *El Paso Inc.* magazine, the *El Paso Times*, the El Paso Writers Guild, Mountain Dreams Publishing, the El Paso Public Library, Texas Western Press and many others also came aboard.

We had about forty tables of authors signing their books, a media row with major publications, book publishers, and live TV coverage throughout the day. There were auctions, raffles, book review lectures, Tigua Indian Dancers, Mexican mariachis, a pottery-making demonstration by former Tigua Indian Governor Albert Alvidrez, and Saint Vincent de Paul had a huge used book sale in the front parking lot. The weather was beautiful and the turnout was HUGE.

The Great Southwest Book Fair and Sale had just about ALL of the best border-area writers including historian Leon Metz, Fred Morales, Lisa Malooly, Frank Mangan and of course superstar Coach Don Haskins.

We had a whole covey of Hillsboro talent including Jan Haley, Max Evans (author of *The Rounders*), artist Robert "Shoofly" Shufelt, Harley Shaw (the world's authority on mountain lions), petroglyph photographer Embree Hale, Jr., and Sue Bason, artist and bookseller.

And there was a very impressive delegation of Texas writers: Bill Crawford, world-famous author of books about border radio, Stevie Ray Vaughan and many other subjects; Tio and Janell Kleberg of the King Ranch; ninety-six-year-old El Pasoan José Cisneros (an internationally acclaimed illustrator); Wyman Meinzer (the official photographer of Texas); and poet Marian Haddad.

And of course, our old friend, Billie Sol Estes was there. The eighty-year-old Texas wheeler-dealer/con man/swindler was sent to prison in 1963 under a cloud of heavy political pressure in the Lyndon Johnson Era. It was interesting to see El Paso's only billionaire buying an autographed book from Billie Sol.

• • •

EVENTS HAVE BECOME an important part of making El Paso Saddleblanket World Headquarters live up to our new slogan: A one-acre shopping ADVENTURE. We have live music on a weekly basis. Many smaller events—pottery-making demonstrations, Indian Trade Markets, pow wows and art shows—also add a lot. All of these events draw people and help your business.

Chapter Twenty-three

The El Paso Saddleblanket Family

*"Bonnie and I don't have kids—just dogs.
Our company is our family."*

MORE THAN THE TRADE GOODS, the travel or the deal making, the most amazing thing about El Paso Saddleblanket has been our employees. Bonnie and I don't have kids. Our employees are our family.

Dennis Rice was our first employee, and he's still working for us. I met Dennis when he was repossesing cars on the Navajo reservation. He's one tough guy, but he is also a champion of the underdog. Whenever I get pissed off at an employee or a customer who isn't measuring up, Dennis says, "Just let me work with him. Just let me work with him." He does. And as far as collections are concerned, it's hard to believe, but our company loses only twenty percent of one percent of total sales. Hell, banks work at a loss rate of one and a half percent of total sales. And that is thanks to our collection man, Dennis.

Dennis, Irma, Carmen, Arah, Maria, JoAnn, Jon, Sergio, Veronica and Frank have all been with us between fifteen and twenty years. In fact, one wall of our office is covered with pictures of our employees' kids. We love it when these kids come to work with us. It makes us feel like we've helped raise them all.

Bonnie feels the same way I do about our El Paso Saddleblanket family. *"Family? Kids? No, we don't have any. Guess we forgot. In our prime childbearing years we were spending so much time in third world countries that having children didn't seem like a good idea. But are we childless? Not exactly. Many of our employees came on board as high schoolers. We have shared their heartbreaks, the thrill of their first cars, the expenses of their weddings and the joy of the arrival of their children. When we want the companionship of a kid we simply invite someone over for a visit. I brag on them as if they were blood relatives. Four of the kids we enjoyed most are now in college. One of the four is an A student at SMU and another is a girl soccer star. I hope someday they look back and find they learned about life or success from Uncle Dusty and Aunt Bonnie. They worked part-time at El Paso Saddleblanket during high school."*

BONNIE CONTINUES TO SET UP scholarship programs for some of the kids who have worked with us. I like to train the kids and our other employees about the business world. What is my motivational technique? Well, nothing formal. Each employee is different, and each one has to be treated differently. Some you've got to really push, and some you've got to stroke and compliment. Most of all, you've got to keep them challenged. Money, of course, is the best motivator. If you can show your employees how they can make more money, they will gladly take your advice and then some.

I love taking our young employees and giving them a chance to succeed. I take these kids to a gift show in Atlanta or Philadelphia, and they go out and make deals with other business people. They're innocent and clean-cut and they do a great job of selling. Most have never flown and some have never stayed in a hotel. Believe me, I've worked hundreds of trade shows over the years, and I can get pretty burnt out. It's great to work with these enthusiastic young kids to keep El Paso Saddleblanket expanding.

For many summers, I chartered a bus and invited all my employees to Rancho El Cid for horseback riding and a mammoth party with a band. It was wild. Once we had 150 guests, all dancing and drinking beer. I also invite my employees to our home in El Paso a few times a year for a poolside party and to a Christmas party at a local hotel. The way we treat each other in the company is so unique that it was written up in the *Wall Street Journal*. Mike Dipp paid me a great compliment once. He said, "Treating people well isn't just business with Dusty and Bonnie. It's above and beyond that. They treat their employees as equals." All I can say is, we try.

OUR CUSTOMERS are also part of our extended family. Most of our customers are independent retailers, folks who own trading posts, small stores or roadside stands. We love our customers because we've been there ourselves. We've sold blankets at flea markets and at roadside stands as well as in showrooms. We know the problems our customers face. We know what products will work for them. And we know that they can succeed with our merchandise.

Desert rats! Yes, God bless them! In our desert here around El Paso and even more so in the New Mexico and Arizona desert live a breed of people we call desert rats. These folks typically live in small camping trailers or old school buses in remote desert areas. They come to town once a week to buy groceries and dump the sewer and fill up the water tanks, etc. Many of these people are artists, craftsmen and traders who work swaps, Indian powwows, street corners and roadsides. We sell to a lot of desert rats and many visit our warehouse. We really appreciate their business and wish them the best of luck.

ONE OF THE FUN THINGS about El Paso Saddleblanket has been the chance to meet a lot of celebrities and other interesting people. In the old days on the road we would work Tucson, Arizona hotel shows during movie making time at the Old Tucson Movie Ranch. Here we met

Steve McQueen and Arnold Schwarzenegger during the shooting of *The Story of Tom Horn* (1978) and *The Villain* (1979). Also actors Ben Johnson, Ken Curtis (Festus on TV's "Gunsmoke"), Slim Pickins, Buddy Hackett, Richard Farnsworth, and Wilford Brimley. Most of these people are very nice and down to earth.

We met even more celebrities when we opened up our retail store in downtown El Paso. For one thing, El Paso is about halfway between Dallas and Phoenix and is a popular place for traveling entertainers to lay over. We have casinos, Juárez night life and lots of things to do. El Paso Saddleblanket had lots of billboards for hundreds of miles in all directions that generated a lot of people traffic. And you'd be surprised how much word of mouth is out there on the road.

Over the years, we've met lots of the musical groups and western stars including Charlie and Hazel Daniels, Brooks & Dunn, Jeanie Frickie, Lenny Kravitz, Metallica, ZZ Top, George Thorogood, Highway 101, Tiny Tim and David Allen Coe. We've also met lots of Latino musicians, bullfighters and various politicians like Texas Governor Ann Richards, Lieutenant Governor Bob Bullock and famous people like Ted Turner and Jane Fonda and many more. Alan Funt came into the store one day. Thank goodness it wasn't a prank. He didn't say, "Smile! You're on candid camera!"

I used to get a little embarrassed when people bothered our celebrity customers with questions and requests for autographs. One day after a lot of gawkers came by the store, I apologized to Charlie Daniels. I'll never forget. He looked me straight in the eyes and said, "Dusty, I worked all of my life so people would ask me for my autograph." He made sure that every employee got an autograph and let them go inside his band's tour buses.

One observation I have made through the years is that most entertainers really, really love their fans and don't seem to mind answering the same questions over and over. I can remember how Steve McQueen used to spend hours hanging around the lobby and the restaurant of the Tucson Hilton just talking to anybody and everybody no matter how squirrelly they might be. He was a huge star at the time and felt very comfortable out milling around and was very patient with people.

It seemed for a while like every day or so we had VIPs visiting the store. For the most part it was a handshake, some small chit chat and then everyone goes about their business, but a few we really got to know through the years.

IN THE SUMMER OF 1976, we were doing our merchandise show at the Santa Fe Hilton when Billy Gibbons of ZZ Top came in and bought some rugs for his Santa Fe home.

After that, the Gibbons place was a regular stop for us and a guaranteed sale. We have kept up with Billy through the years and he comes to El Paso on a fairly regular basis.

We used to sell these sheepskin rugs that were sewn together like the large hide outline of a polar bear. They were really neat. They looked like a real polar bear. Billy liked these rugs real well. He called us from somewhere in Europe while he was on tour and ordered a bunch of these rugs to be sent out to different women. "Send one to Gigi in Paris, Lola in Rome, Heidi in Germany…"

Billy is quite a sport with the women and everyone liked him. He's easy to be around and handles his fans gracefully, always in total control. A short time ago he called from Los Angeles and told me that his new passion is collecting some kind of African headwear and primitive sculpture. He's been spending quite a bit of time in Africa lately, collecting.

LATE ONE NIGHT during the Christmas season of 1988, Andy Williams came into town for a concert. He was riding in a limo on the way from the airport to his hotel when he passed by El Paso Saddleblanket and noticed one of our large inside window neon signs had a pretty big electrical fire. He had the driver call the police and the fire department and insisted on staying until everything was taken care of.

The next day we went over to his dressing room and personally thanked him and gave him a saddleblanket as a token of our appreciation for possibly saving the store from burning. He came over later and we learned that he was a hard-core collector of Indian rugs. We plan to visit him soon at the Andy Williams Theater in Branson, Missouri.

IN 1983, we formed a business partnership with two old famous rodeo performers from the 1940s and 1950s: All-around Rodeo Cowboy Champion Casey Tibbs and 1948 and 1951 World Champion Bronc Rider Gerald Roberts of Abilene, Kansas. The deal was that El Paso Saddleblanket would furnish and fund the leather and hair-on cowhides and sell our new product, "Casey Tibbs Cowboy Chaps." Gerald had a small factory to make the chaps in Abilene, Kansas, and he did the designs and manufacturing. We all loved Casey, but I'm still not sure what he really did for the business (except keeping all of us entertained). I don't think we ever made much money, but it was some fun times indeed. Bonnie and I were hard working and very ambitious "kids" in our thirties and Gerald and Casey were still crazy wild old cowboys in their seventies.

We were together many years and one day we learned that Casey was dying of cancer. Charlie Daniels and actor Richard Farnsworth decided that we should all work on raising money for a one-and-a-half size bronze statue of Casey riding a bull to be put in front of the National Rodeo Hall of Fame in Colorado Springs, Colorado. Charlie and Richard recruited us along with tons of folks in the rodeo and entertainment business to work on this project. They organized a huge celebrity fundraising party at the Beverly Hills Hilton Hotel in Beverly Hills, California. This was both the greatest and saddest event I have ever been directly involved in. We worked a lot setting everything up and HOLLYWOOD CAME! Gene Autry, Roy Rogers, Rex Allen and on and on. EVERYBODY who ever sang a cowboy song or played in a western movie showed up. El Paso Saddleblanket made a big Casey Tibbs rug with his name on it that sold for $5,000 in the benefit auction. We sold some of Casey's old cowboy boots and his famous purple shirts for huge amounts. Charlie Daniels and all the Nashville crowd put on a hell of a show. We easily raised enough money that night to more than pay for the bronze statue. Casey was pretty sick by the time we had the party, but came through like a true champion. He died not long after that at his ranch in Ramona, California. If you're ever in Colorado Springs, please visit the Rodeo Hall of Fame and see Casey's statue. It's beautiful, and we're all very proud of it.

RENE RENE was a Latino music star back in the 1960s and was one of the first entertainers to record bilingual, English-Spanish, music in a big way. Rene used to spend a lot of time in El Paso and was extremely popular here, so we got to know him very well. He liked to come to our house and play the piano and sing along with our howling German shepherds.

WE GOT TO KNOW the Texas Tornadoes pretty well through the years: Freddie Fender, Flaco Jiménez, Augie Meyers and Doug Sahm. We had a great old 1959 Cadillac limo that we loaned them every time they were in El Paso. One day while cruising around with Freddie and the guys, the limo conked out. No problem! Freddie rolled up his sleeves, dug in and fixed the problem. He was a mechanic in South Texas before becoming famous.

Another limo story. One time there was a big celebration in El Paso for Father Rahm, a local priest who had devoted his life to working with the poor. Father Rahm was, and still is, revered as almost a saint here in El Paso. Anyway, the city renamed a street in south El Paso after Father Rahm and threw a parade in his honor. It was a big, big deal here. I loaned them the limo to drive Father Rahm in the parade. It was very hot that day, and we had no AC. To make things worse, the limo heated up and stalled out in the middle of the parade! The parade was live on TV, and the limo stalled out right in front of the TV cameras with our logo painted big on the side. A lot of people kidded me about that, but I swear it was an accident. The limo sat there, blocking the parade, until Father Rahm finally got out and started walking. Eventually, we got the old limo running again and gave Father Rahm the tribute he truly deserved.

• • •

ONE OF MY FAVORITE celebrity friends is Billie Sol Estes. Billie Sol is one of the most notorious wheeler-dealers in Texas history, who hustled everything from surplus Army barracks to cotton allotments to anhydrous ammonia before he went to prison. "Everybody has a little bit of wheeler-dealer in him trying to get out," says Billie Sol, who's been a free man living in Granbury, Texas since 1984.

I've always admired Billie Sol for some reason or other. I guess I just admire the fact that he is a masterful deal maker, although some of his deals didn't turn out so well. One of the most interesting things about Billie Sol is that he has absolutely no ego. Instead of telling you how great he is, he likes to tell you how great you are. Many folks in Texas revere him as some kind of folk hero, like Robin Hood or Jesse James.

A few years back, I invited Billie Sol into El Paso and got him on a popular radio talk show hosted by my friend Paul Strelzin. They were talking along, when Billie Sol announced that he was going on a national tour to give his money away—and that he was going to start his tour at the H & H Carwash in El Paso at 10 A.M. the following day. Everyone was surprised to hear that, especially my friends Kenny and Maynard Haddad who own the carwash. Well, a big crowd gathered to see what was going to happen. Billie Sol didn't give all his money away, but he did give away a stack of two dollar bills and autographed each one, "I've been swindled by Billie Sol Estes…"

Chapter Twenty-four

Retire? Never!

"Have fun and make $$$."

I'VE BEEN CALLED a lot of things over the years, and many of them I can't put into print. But one thing I have been called is one of the best marketers on the border. That means a lot. The border is a tough place to cut a deal and a tough place to survive. We've not only survived on the border—we've thrived. I guess by most people's definition we are self-made since we started out selling saddleblankets and rugs out of the back of a pick-up truck and built that into a multimillion dollar business. Although I proudly have never asked for or received business financial backing from anyone, I have had an abundance of help in the way of advice, encouragement and support from family, friends and even complete strangers.

Our life has been blessed with opportunity, luck and travel experiences that only a few people will ever have. I do not believe that anyone on earth is completely self-made because we have all had some help whether it be from a friend, an uncle, school teacher, coach or someone else along the way. We are no exception. We love the border with all its charm, adventure, danger, romance and dark sides. One of the best selling

T-shirts at the store pictures a .38 revolver pistol with the caption "El Paso, Texas, Its Ain't Kansas."

Every day I get questions. Lots of questions like: What would you change? What's your secret to doing business? Any advice for a new-comer in the business? How are your dogs? Are you ever going to retire or sell the El Paso Saddleblanket Company? What are your hobbies? Religion? Politics? Business philosophies? How, where, what, could you suggest I buy or sell or whatever? Who or what do you admire or dislike? What is best, where is best (or worst)? What should I do?

I think I know the answers to most of these questions.

A good catchall answer to most of the advice questions would be: "That depends" or "I'm not sure." I like to put a disclaimer on most every-thing else by saying, "I'm not saying what you should do, but this is what I might consider doing."

On a personal note, I would like to leave you with some of my thoughts and views on a range of subjects, mainly business related. I usually start off my day at about 6:30 A.M. sitting at the computer in my jockey shorts sipping coffee, checking e-mails that might have come in overnight from Asia or Europe and seeing how many catalog requests I got from insom-niacs. I play with my German shepherds, go to the store, come home, play with the dogs and then go back and work in my office at home until bedtime. I work more than ever now and I love it more than ever. I do not care for much personal publicity and do not feel very comfortable at social events. I have never spoken publicly at any event nor have I ever featured myself in any of the thousands of our radio and TV commercials. Bonnie is the same. I just love to promote my business.

El Paso Saddleblanket is my alter ego and it's HUGE.

OUR DOGS are also a big part of the El Paso Saddleblanket family. Nowa-days, we have El Cid III and Bobbi. They are quite a handful, but we feel like they take care of us as much as we take care of them.

Even after nearly forty years, I still enjoy visiting trading posts across the country. I recently called on some of our old trading post customers in Gallup, New Mexico on the Navajo Indian Reservation. Wow, what great country and what great people! Unlike Santa Fe or Scottsdale, Gallup is a wholesale town. Folks come into Gallup from all over the world to buy from the hundreds of turquoise Indian jewelry stores in the area.

On this recent trip, I sold a lot of the wool trade blankets, doubleweave saddleblankets, cowhides and Mexican saddles to the Indian traders. The old Route 66 highway stores were buying a lot of our small stenciled place mats, scorpion paperweights and other tourist curio items. Lots of the gas stations and curio stores give away our inexpensive arrowheads with a fill-up or a purchase over $10. Works for them! I get a big kick out of seeing all the giant highway billboards promoting our nine cent arrowheads, "Three for $5!"

It made me happy and proud to realize that our merchandise is still popular on Route 66. You know that if you are still selling to the same clients for this many years, you are doing something right. That is the best way to run a business. Get customers and keep them. Our customers are as much a part of El Paso Saddleblanket as we are. We weave together suppliers, designers, products and retailers, just as our craftsmen in Juárez weave together fine rugs. In 1994 we wrote a book for our customers called *How To Start and Operate Your Own Southwest Store and Trading Post.* We wrote the book in five days in a New York City hotel room during a winter snow storm. It is now available for free over the internet at www.elpasosaddleblanket.com.

TODAY it is so much easier to start your business than it was when we were starting out. We have the best selection, the best designs, the best prices, and you can receive your orders faster than ever before. Our business is always better during economic downturns because we can offer customers better quality at lower prices. We are reliable traders who have been in business for almost forty years. We don't cheat or play games with prices. No get rich promises. No franchise fees. No phony sales kits. No hype. Just proven quality, beautiful merchandise that has been selling steady for years.

I firmly believe that no matter how sophisticated technology gets, and no matter how far the world reaches into cyberspace, people will always have a special appreciation for works of beauty that are shaped by the hands of artisans using centuries-old skills and techniques passed down from their elders.

The reproduction of age-old crafts fulfills two very important functions that connect the past to the future:

1. It is a powerful transmitter of culture from one generation to the next.
2. It allows artisans to improve their lot in life with better health care, education and communication with other segments of society.

As traders, we help connect the past to the present. We fulfill the needs of consumers, we make a good living for ourselves, and we send money down the line to support hundreds of artists and craftspeople. I don't ever tire of saying HANDwoven, HANDpainted, HANDmade and HANDcrafted because this is the very essence of what makes Southwest merchandise so special. Thank goodness there are no computerized machines that can duplicate these crafts.

I promise you one thing. If you call El Paso Saddleblanket, you will always talk to a real live person and never some fuckin' answering machine.

I'M GETTING OLDER now (I was born in 1944, you can do the math). With as many miles as I have on me, I sometimes wish I was a little wiser than I am. Our life has pretty much been focused on business and I have only limited interest in a few other things. I don't have hobbies. I don't follow sports. I don't have much close family (Bonnie has no living family). I don't go to church. I don't socialize very much. We are not members of any country club, service club, organized religion or political party. We don't gamble, don't have or want kids, and rarely watch TV or read newspapers. Therefore I do not feel qualified to expand on a range of subjects.

• • •

ONE OF THE THINGS I get asked about is the import business. All I can say is that the overwhelming majority of the people that enter this business fail. Why is this? Well, most people get into importing by making wishful, emotional decisions with total disregard for practical application. I have seen the same scenario play out hundreds of times here on the border with non-thinking dreamers who fantasize about setting up their own little arts and crafts empire in Mexico or some other country and being the great savior of all these poor ignorant people while getting rich just because they have "discovered" some village that produces some product.

I know that in Mexico, the Mexicans call these people the "Lorenzos." as in *Lawrence of Arabia*, the movie where the white-guy savior goes and leads all these Arabs to victory. These are usually phony ultra-liberal types who see themselves as heroes and self-appointed crusaders saving a culture. These amateur Lorenzos end up paying too much for the products and have absolutely no clue or plan on marketing. These people are fools.

I believe first you should come up with a business plan to SELL whatever item you might have, since anyone with any money can eventually figure out where to purchase any given product at the right price. It is my belief that importing should be ninety percent about selling and ten percent about buying. Ask yourself, "Am I going to wholesale the merchandise or am I going to sell it retail?" If you don't know the answer to this, it should tell you that you should not get into this business.

Let's now go to practical application. If you plan to import items to sell retail, chances are that you could not purchase enough to make it worthwhile. And you don't need an eight-year supply, even if you get a very good price. A lot of things like packing, freight, customs broker fees in both the U.S. and Mexico, duties, breakage, shortages, your travel expenses and much more need to be factored into the total landed cost of the goods. (And this assumes you don't get ripped off somewhere along the way.) So if you are thinking about direct import to sell retail at your store or local flea market, I suggest you carefully consider these things.

The wholesale business for importers is much, much more difficult. Did you ever hear the saying "You don't go to Kansas to buy seafood"? Even if it has good prices, the fact that a company is located in the Midwest suggests that it may not be the best source in many people's mind. Wholesale is a competitive, dog-eat-dog business. You must be competitive and also learn to make a profit if you wish to stay in business. You need to have large warehouse facilities, a reliable pipeline of goods and provide credit to wholesale customers. There is a balance of buying to maintain. If you don't sell enough to keep your workers employed, you lose your sources.

Language is certainly a challenge. How do you advertise for wholesale? Again, my theory is that it's all about selling. And when you get bogged down with other things, it most certainly cuts into your selling time. Sales are what pull the train and without sales you can sink very fast. This is the mistake that the Lorenzos always make.

OK, so what's the answer to someone who wants to sell imported items? I say that it's possible to get into the direct import business at some time, but first I suggest that it is probably more cost-effective at the start to pay a little more for the product from an established company that already has the goods so you can concentrate on the selling end. Keep on selling and listening to your business, you'll know when it's time to direct import. No need to hurry.

Another thing to keep in mind is the products. For example a tourist will come here to the border and go the Juárez Mercado, have a couple of beers, buy some pink and green donkey trinket, but that does not mean these products will sell well in Buffalo, New York or Seattle.

Gotta be careful not to get stuck with crap that won't move.

As I LOOK INTO my crystal ball, my gut feeling is that things aren't going well for our country, therefore we need to be smarter and figure out how to be on the winning side. Remember, there's always someone who makes money. In wars, it's the people who sell guns. After a hail storm the roofers make money. In a depression, buy a liquor store because people drink more.

In our wholesale business there are less stores to sell to because there are less stores. Now in the small towns throughout the U.S. small stores are closing everyday because Wal-Mart, Target and other "big-box" stores are coming in with huge stores with lower prices and sucking in business from a fifty-mile radius. The standard mom-and-pop stores are closing.

So what can be done to combat this trend? One thing we did was convince the stores still operating to handle more of our merchandise. We have a unique product niche and we do not sell to the big-box stores. Our pitch is "Hey, if you want to be in business for yourself, you gotta sell something, so why not stock and sell more of our products?"

Another thing was to find (and/or create) more independent dealers or event sales vendors. We also successfully targeted the online and E-bay sellers. Judging from the size of their orders, our customers who sell online are doing VERY well. You can't give up. You just need to change with the times. We target more international customers now since the dollar is weaker, making our products cheaper for them.

So get tough, think positive, change with the times and try to stay ahead of the game.

It seems that it was just not that long ago when we were a young married couple out on the road chasing the American dream: working, playing, traveling, selling, having a good time and loving it all. I must admit that for the most part, even though we had some disappointments, we were very fortunate to have lived in the times we did. Luck was on our side. We worked very hard. We were honest and honorable in our business dealings. We had very little interest in anything else but our business. Yes, all that counts toward success, but I will always believe in sheer luck. If a business goes bad, you can't always personally blame yourself and when a business does extremely well, you can't always personally take all the credit.

EL PASO SADDLEBLANKET keeps evolving, and we enjoy evolving with it. How do we combine our work and our marriage? I don't know. Maybe Bonnie can explain better than I can.

"We are with each other twenty-four hours a day every day, entertaining, and relaxing, but most of all working from the time we get up until the time we go to sleep. Most married couples could not endure our 24-7 schedule. But somehow it works for us.

"Both of us are constantly thinking business. Someone asked if we ever take a vacation. No need, really. Every business trip is part vacation. Every day at the office is part vacation. We love spending time with our dogs, going to lunch with friends, etcetera. We would be bored to tears if we were isolated from our business. Some of the nicest people I've ever met are our customers and our employees. Its all kind of a far flung yet closely knit family.

"I can't imagine ever retiring. Dusty and I go to the warehouse every day except when we are gone on business trips to South America, Europe, Africa, India and Asia. We make at least twenty trips to various places in Mexico every year as we have been doing for many, many years. It's always a busy schedule. But it's our life, we love what we do and can't imagine doing anything else."

ONE THING ABOUT GETTING OLDER, I am more cynical, less trusting and less impressed with people's money, especially those who did not earn it themselves. Nothing much surprises me. I got very callused after eighteen years in downtown El Paso with all the scammers, hookers, pimps and drug dealers—not to mention all the phony necktie-wearing, Chamber-of-Commerce-type sons of bitches.

I feel very fortunate to have had a great father, uncles, cousins and family friends that go back a long time. We have met some great people through the years. Unfortunately many are not active now and many are not around any more. Many of the old traders we knew from Juárez, the trade shows, Route 66 and the reservation have passed on including Maxie and Gilbert Ortega, Manny Goodman, Dave Candelaria, Mauricio Sidransky and Nudie of West Hollywood, California. Former El Paso Mayor Jon Rogers, the banker who loaned us millions of dollars over the years is gone. Uncle Shorty passed away in Abilene. We carried him the last mile to the Henson Cemetery on Uncle Arthel's ranch in his favorite means of transportation: a horse-drawn wagon.

• • •

AFTER A BRIEF ILLNESS, my father Mack Henson, age eighty-four, passed away peacefully at home on December 26, 2004. One hour after his death the huge tsunami hit in Asia. I couldn't help but to think, "Wow, what a big send off!" Mack's funeral was mostly a party with a Western Band, the way we thought he would like to be remembered. I think you will enjoy the article about him in the back of this book.

My mother died peacefully at home the next year.

I'm proud that my dad was an independent businessman who never retired. The idea of working for a boss and then retiring never made any sense to him, and it never made any sense to me. I'm proud of my work, my wife, my employees, my customers and my vendors. Trading is not only my business, it's my life. And it's a great life. Bonnie has enjoyed it just as much as I have, though as she explains below, it hasn't always been easy.

"I'm not sure that the life we have had and the business we have built could ever be duplicated. It's been great fun, but I wouldn't want to have to start over. As many incidents in this book demonstrate, we didn't do everything right. Dusty just has the knack of turning a challenge into something new and interesting. I haven't always been happy about some of the situations we've gotten INTO, but I'm continually amazed at Dusty's ability to get us OUT OF a bad situation. He never stops thinking and planning. It's so hard to write a closing chapter to our story because I don't know what we might get into in the years ahead. I know there's still a big project out there, just waiting for us."

RETIRE? NEVER! Why would Bonnie and I ever retire from work that we love? We still aren't finished living the amazing story of El Paso Saddleblanket Company.

It's like when a customer in the store asked me recently, "Dusty, have you lived in Texas all your life?"

"…Not yet."

A Tribute to My Dad, Mack Henson

MAXIE AQUILLA HENSON was born in a tent in Ranger Hill, Texas on July 10, 1920 during the Ranger oil boom. Mack, as his parents called him, was the third of five children born to Claude Jackson Henson and his wife Olive Lutrell Henson. Both C.J.—as he was called—and Olive were born in Texas in the 1800s.

Mack Henson went to school in Seymour, Texas during the lean years of the Great Depression. He dropped out of school at age twelve to help support the family. He sold newspapers, shined shoes and did odd jobs. It was

Mack Henson

hard times, but young Mack Henson did pretty well, relying on his natural instincts, charm and street smarts. He was curious and an adventurer. By the time he was fifteen, Mack and his brother Shorty had ridden freight trains several times to California where they worked in construction, picked grapes and worked as kitchen helpers.

In 1936 at age sixteen, Mack went to work for Jake and Troy Wells at their Seymour Café in Seymour, Texas. Mack became a short-order cook and excelled at baking fruit pies. The Wells brothers became his mentors and

Mack was an eager apprentice. For the rest of his life, Mack would be involved in the restaurant business one way or another.

But Mack could never turn down a challenge. In 1938, he joined a crew of door-to-door salesmen peddling magazine subscriptions all over the midwestern United States. He prospered in this business and was soon in charge of the crew even though he was the youngest. Since it was the Dust Bowl era and money was scarce, Mack sometimes promoted payments for his subscriptions from rural farmers in goods rather than cash. Mack particularly liked old gold teeth and live chickens. He even built a chicken cage on top of his car to carry his earnings.

In the late 1930s, C.J. and the entire Henson clan moved to Abilene, Texas. C.J. and Mack's older brother Arthel went to work in the Paymaster Feed Mill. C.J. worked the night shift and ran a small roadside produce stand during the day. C.J. liked to sleep in his chair next to the stand. When a customer wanted something they just woke him up. Times were a little different back then. Eventually, C.J. opened a small grocery store that became an Abilene institution.

In the prewar days of the early 1940s, the military began building army bases around the country. A construction boom came to the Abilene area with the building of Camp Barkly in nearby View, Texas. At age twenty Mack and his partner Bill Bailey borrowed money, purchased an old trailer house and turned it into a small diner. Mack and Bill started serving hamburgers and chili to the hungry hoards of construction workers. Mack lived in a converted chicken coop behind the trailer house diner. Bill hired a local farm girl by the name of Roma Jean Richards as a waitress. When the young waitress met the busy short-order cook, his first words to her were "Get the hell out of my kitchen." Mack and Jean married in the spring of 1941 and stayed married for over sixty years.

I guess Mack said the right thing to her after all.

W HEN the Camp Barkly construction work was finished, Mack closed the trailer house café with no name. He finagled a job as the construction foreman on another military camp to be built in Leadville, Colorado, and the newlyweds moved to Leadville. Mack excelled in the construction business but was drafted into the Army after just a few months in Leadville.

Mack went to Jefferson Barracks Military Post in Missouri for basic training, then on to Spokane, Washington and March Field, California where he waited to be shipped out for combat in the South Pacific. Only hours before

Mack's First Grocery Store in North Abilene, Texas, 1946.

his military unit was to be shipped out, his brother Shorty was in a terrible train accident near Houston. Mack got an emergency furlough to see Shorty, who was in critical condition. When Mack returned to March Field his company had shipped out. Mack learned later that almost all of the soldiers in his outfit were killed in action.

Mack was reassigned to the Army Air Corps bombing range near Tonopah, Nevada where he set up both day and night targets for B-25 bombing practice.

Mack did very well in Tonopah and soon made the rank of sergeant. He and Jean purchased a building on the main street and opened The Quick Way Photo portrait studio where he took and sold portrait photos to soldiers. This was wide open Nevada in the 1940s and it suited Mack just fine. They installed slot machines in the studio. He bought and sold motorcycles, cars and items that were in short supply during war time—gasoline, nylons and other things. Mack also loaned money and operated an informal pawn service. He became a very good poker player, a passion that lasted throughout the rest of his life. Things in Tonopah were good for Mack. He even built a small house using mostly scrap materials from the bombing range. In the war years soldiers inspected and rode on the hoods of people's cars as they drove across Hoover Dam. Mack smuggled untaxed whiskey across the dam by hiding it under the baby crib of his new born son, Dusty.

Mack and Jean Henson would have probably stayed in Nevada if it wasn't for Mack's family back in Texas. Sure enough, in 1945, after the war, Mack and Jean returned to Abilene. Mack opened up a café, ran it for a short time and sold it. He and brother Shorty did cement contracting for a brief time.

In 1946, Mack took the $600 he had saved up in the Army and used this to open Mack Henson Grocery & Meat, his first small grocery store in North Abilene.

*Mack Henson with Dusty
(on left) and Bennie, fishing
Fort Phantom Lake, Abilene,
Texas, June 6, 1951.*

The postwar era of the late 1940s and early 1950s were prosperous times in America. Mack's family grew as did his business. Son Bennie was born in 1947, and daughter Melba in 1950. Between 1946 and 1954 Mack doubled the size of his grocery about every two years. By 1954, Mack Henson Grocery & Meat was selling clothing and hardware. His store included a jewelry shop and watch repair, a barber shop and even offered dry cleaning pick-up and delivery. This kind of one stop shopping was the basic concept that Wal-mart and K-mart use today. Mack Henson was doing it fifty years ago in Abilene, Texas. Mack, his sister Louise and her husband Jake Cagle opened a gas station and salvage yard. Dusty had a snow cone stand in the parking lot.

Mack even had his own fifteen-minute TV show that aired every Wednesday. And Mack appeared as the master of ceremonies at many functions in and around Abilene. All the Henson siblings—Mack, Arthel, Shorty, Melvin and sister Louise—did well during this time. The brothers owned neighboring cabins on Fort Phantom Lake. Mack swam two miles across the lake on his thirtieth birthday, July 10, 1950.

Life was good!

BUT MACK didn't lay back and take things easy. In 1955 and 1956 he opened three convenience stores, the Quickway Stores, in Abilene. He built a small strip center east of the big store which included Hawkeye's Diner and the latest fad in Abilene—a coin-operated laundry.

In 1957, Mack sold the Quickway Stores and some rent houses, leased the big store to Wooten Grocery Company and retired at age thirty-seven.

Mack hunted, fished, traveled some, managed his properties and piddled in other small business deals. But he got restless. So in 1959, he made a deal with the General Electric Company to open coin-operated laundries featuring GE machines nationwide. It was a sweet deal for Mack. He had the full financial backing of GE and took many trips scouting locations for this promising new business. The first three laundries were scheduled to open in Alamosa, Monte Vista and Del Norte, three small towns in the San Luis Valley of Southern Colorado. On a cold Sunday in February 1959 just before signing the papers for the first new GE coin-operated laundry in Colorado, Mack and Jean drove up to Wolf Creek Pass and passed a beautiful ranch along the banks of the Rio Grande River, five miles west of South Fork, Colorado. They noticed that the ranch was for sale. Instead of signing the papers for the coin-operated laundries, Mack and Jean signed a contract to buy his dream ranch, the ranch that we all know today as Fun Valley.

In May of 1959, the Henson Family and long-time employees Jackie Woods, Jeanie Woods and Cleve Bilbrey left Abilene for Colorado. By the end of that summer, Fun Valley was open for business. The ranch featured a miniature golf course, a commercial trout fishing pond and horse rentals. By the fall of 1959 Mack had his Colorado outfitter guide license and had established a camp in the mountains for hunters.

In 1960 bulldozers were clearing land and building lakes at Fun Valley. Although over one hundred people had previously been turned down, Mack applied for a liquor license. Somehow, Mack got his license, the first liquor license of this type issued in Rio Grande County. Mack and Jean opened the Fun Valley Steakhouse and Bar. The opening was a huge success, featuring Slim Willett, a friend and famous Abilene Western singer who wrote the 1950s smash hit "Don't Let the Stars Get in Your Eyes." During the summer of 1960, other entertainers including Johnnie Lee Wills, the brother of Bob Wills, also performed at the Fun Valley Steakhouse and Bar.

During the 1960s, Mack didn't slow down at all. He got himself elected president of the South Fork Chamber of Commerce. He got together with South Fork restaurant owner Jimmy Minter. Together, Mack and Jimmie organized the Rio Grande World Champion Raft Race, which was a huge success.

Mack built a motel at Fun Valley in the spring of 1961. In the spring of 1962, Mack and Jean constructed a roller skating rink and some rental cabins on the river.

The expansion at Fun Valley was successful but tough. After the winter of

1959–1960, the Hensons moved their base of operations back to Texas and every year opened Fun Valley from May through November. In 1968 Mack bought the Spruce Ski Lodge in South Fork and the El Rio Hotel in Del Norte. He changed the name of the El Rio to The Old West Hotel. In 1970, he transformed the hotel into an Old-West-themed Trading Post Mall, featuring ten stores including the James Richards Pottery Shop. In 1971, Mack bought three more buildings and a small ranch in Del Norte, Colorado.

In the early '70s all the Henson children, Dusty, Bennie and Melba got involved in the family business. And the Henson family continued to grow. Melba had two children, Kyle and Molly. Bennie had two sons, Mack David and Henk. Dusty stayed single until age thirty and had no children.

Throughout the 1970s, Mack continued to expand the Fun Valley RV Park until it reached about five hundred spaces. He built a "Funitorium" that featured live entertainment every night. He changed the skating rink into a square-dance barn and a few years later, Mack built a big new square-dance barn on the river. Fun Valley now included twenty-seven man-made lakes in addition to a mile-and-a-half of the Rio Grande River.

The late 1970s and early 1980s were great times for the Hensons. Having raised up their kids, Mack and Jean ran Fun Valley every summer. In the winter season, they spent much time traveling to Las Vegas and taking fishing trips to Mexico.

Back in Abilene, Mack launched several new careers. He took up oil painting. He specialized in landscapes and quickly sold everything he painted. Mack was flattered when one of his paintings was stolen from Fun Valley.

Mack was always a showman. He performed in several community theater plays in Abilene and had small parts in two different movies that were filmed in Las Vegas. Mack enjoyed going to the disc jockey convention in Nashville to book and promote acts for the Fun Valley Funatorium. He traveled to Europe and South America. He hired an agent and spent some time in Hollywood making the rounds. He had a very hard time accepting the fact that Hollywood was not particularly interested in an actor in his sixties with limited experience. Nevertheless, he somehow got his Screen Actors Guild card.

In 1987 at age sixty-seven, Mack moved from Abilene and bought a new home on Lake Granbury in Granbury, Texas. He bought a store on the Granbury Town Square and some property on Highway 377 where he promptly put in an RV Park and opened the Cowboy Market Place Gift Store and Trading Post. Bennie managed the Granbury property. Melba managed Fun Valley and the Colorado properties. Dusty left in 1974 to start his own business, the El Paso Saddleblanket Company.

At about this time, Mack took up the game of golf. He played whenever he could, even well into his eighties. He really enjoyed his Fun Valley golfing buddies.

In the late 1980s and 1990s, Mack spent more and more time playing poker in Las Vegas. He hung out with "Amarillo Slim" the gambler, some of his Hollywood friends and others. Mack became a well-known and respected gambler at the MGM Grand. He played in the World Series of Poker at

Mack Henson, making a wonderful life out of the cards he was dealt.

Binion's Horseshoe. Some of his poker games were twenty-four and thirty-six-hour ordeals and he loved them. After age seventy-five, Mack began to slow some but enjoyed Fun Valley, his family, his customers, employees and friends more than ever.

Many of you probably remember the HUGE eightieth birthday party we threw for Mack Henson at Fun Valley on July 10, 2000. We turned off all the lights and over two thousand people lit candles and sang "Happy Birthday" to Mack. It was very moving.

In later years, Mack and Jean liked to cruise Fun Valley in their golf cart greeting customers and children, spreading happiness and joy wherever they went. In fact, you could say Mack spent his whole life spreading happiness and joy wherever he went. Mack Henson was an adventurer, a businessman, a soldier, an entrepreneur, a gambler and a bit of an outlaw who touched the lives of folks from Abilene to Tonopah to Fun Valley to Las Vegas to Granbury to Mexico.

Mack Henson was a fine man who led an amazing life.